CW01084863

FERRARI

A MEMORY

FERRARI

A MEMORY

by Gino Rancati

Motorbooks International
Publishers & Wholesalers Inc
Osceola, Wisconsin 54020, USA   ®

This edition first published in 1989 by
Motorbooks International Publishers &
Wholesalers Inc, P O Box 2, 729
Prospect Avenue, Osceola, WI 54020
USA. This edition not for sale in the
UK, Australia and New Zealand

© Gino Rancati, 1989

All rights reserved. With the exception
of quoting brief passages for the
purposes of review no part of this
publication may be reproduced without
prior written permission from the
publisher

Motorbooks International is a certified
trademark, registered with the United
States Patent Office

Printed and bound in the United States
of America

The information in this book is true
and complete to the best of our
knowledge. All recommendations are
made without any guarantee on the part
of the author or publisher, who also
disclaim any liability incurred in
connection with the use of this data or
specific details

We recognize that some words, model
names and designations, for example,
mentioned herein are the property of
the trademark holder. We use them for
identification purposes only. This is not
an official publication

**Library of Congress Cataloging-in-
Publication Data**
Rancati, Gino.
  [Ferrari, l'unico. English]
  Ferrari, a memory / Gino Rancati.
  Translation of: Ferrari, l'unico.
  Bibliography: p.
  Includes index.
  ISBN 0-87938-339-9
  1. Ferrari, Enzo,
1898–1988.   2. Automobile
engineers—Italy—Biography.   I. Title.
TL140.F48R3813   1989
629.2'092'4—dc19   88-31187
[B]   CIP

On the front cover: Enzo Ferrari.
Franco Villani The Ferrari F40. *Pirelli
Tire Corporation*
On the back cover: Enzo Ferrari, a
unique individual.

Motorbooks International books are
also available at discounts in bulk
quantity for industrial or sales-
promotional use. For details write to
Special Sales Manager at the Publisher's
address

Contents

Gentile Rancoati,

Grazie per le sua affettuosa, comprensiva lettera.

Non posso più offrire importanza alcuna a critiche e rilievi; dopo quelle che ho provato è troppo mi appare irrilevante quanto, in passato, formava ragione di vivere disappunto e replica.

Vado in fondo a questa stagione prossima poi ho deciso di lasciare ad altri d'amore di meglio difendere il pre e stigio del lavoro italiano all'estero.

Bisogna sapere rinunciare nella vita quello che ci preme vere, mette ed io penso che, dopo aver perduto mio figlio, io non possa e non abbia nulla di più caro da rinunciare.

Spero di vederla presto e sente cari saluti.

[signature]

16/7/56
Modena

(Translation appears in text of page 77)

Prologue

D ino Ferrari died in Modena on the 30th June 1956. He was born on the 19th January 1932 and baptized Alfredo.

On the 1st July, the day after Ferrari's young son had passed away, the French Grand Prix – a Formula 1 world championship round – was held at Reims. The Ferraris were there at the start: that was what the drivers of the scuderia wanted. The winner was in fact a single-seater from Modena, driven by Peter Collins. Eugenio Castellotti came second and Juan Manuel Fangio came fourth, both of them also driving the Cavallino's cars. Poor Dino was thus honoured by his father's drivers.

In the middle of July, I received a letter shown on the previous page (a translation appears on page 79).

Towards the end of 1956, the Maranello lion was already preparing for the battles of the following year. His intention of quitting, which he confided to me in his letter in July, had been forgotten. If he had carried it out, he would not have been called Ferrari.

This man, who is unique in the history of the motor-car, lived for racing, for the cars which he considered to be creatures, lived to show everyone what he was made of and lived to avenge himself on those who may have doubted his abilities and resources. These qualities have led him to be known throughout the world as 'Ferrari'.

Though his son was dead, he would continue to live for racing. Years later, when he had become even richer and even more famous, he needed the races even more. It was as if they provided artificial 'paradises' for him.

As he gradually climbed higher and higher, he never forgot what his father had told him, namely that companies function properly when the number of associates is unequal and less than three. Thus there would be no such companies. He, Ferrari, would be enough on his own. However, things turned out differently and the old, indomitable lion ended up in a gilded cage. But he still had his scuderia and his races, which gave him the independence, the freedom and the will to do as he saw fit. Until, in the summer of 1988 . . .

1

But who is Enzo Ferrari from Modena ?

O n the 30 June 1960, Ferrari wrote me a note in violet ink: 'Dear Signor Gino, Thank you. See you on the evening of the sixth. Ferrari.' On the 2 July, I received another note, also written by hand – which is what he would do when he didn't want his secretaries to see – saying: 'Thank you for the consignment. See you on the sixth. Ferrari.'

The 'consignment' referred to was red wine, to go with the strawberries that Ferrari enjoyed so much. The wine was sent to him by my father, who had selected it with his customary care. Two notes in three days, and both of them with a rendezvous for the evening of the sixth. One day later – Wednesday the 7 July – was to be an important date: the University of Bologna was to grant Enzo Ferrari an honorary degree in mechanical engineering. Ferrari wanted me to go to Bologna with him and be his only companion at the ceremony. I now sometimes wonder whether he really needed me there or whether he asked me as a reward for my affection for him?

Maranello, 7 July. We had breakfast together at the Cavallino, the famous restaurant opposite the factory, which the *Commendatore* [Italian for 'commander' – an Italian order of chivalry] always expected to be run in an exemplary manner. Peppino, his faithful driver and general helper was ready to leave for Bologna. Suddenly, Ferrari asked me: 'Which car shall we take?' Less than a year before he had treated himself to a Ferrari.

In recent years, he had travelled for six months in a Fiat, six months in a Lancia and six months in an Alfa Romeo, so as not to hurt anyone's feelings. But now he had a Ferrari, properly paid for

– about five million lire, I think. Gerolamo Gardini, the factory's sales manager, had required the payment, but had given him a discount, though it was a small one. This was during the period when everything had been supervised by Ferrari in person. A driver needing fuel to test a car or to go on a trip had to present himself at the factory's filling station with a slip bearing the Commendatore's signed approval.

I replied to his question by suggesting the Ferrari, to which he said: 'What about the professors? They may be arriving on foot and if they see me pull up in a car worth five million . . . No, not the Ferrari.'

At that time, the Commendatore also had a Peugeot 404, which belonged to a brother-in-law in Lyon. I had never understood what use it was to him.

Since the Ferrari was obviously out of the question, I fell back on the Peugeot. 'Nice idea, Gino. An Italian university awards me a degree and I go to collect it in a foreign car! A fine impression that will make. No, not the Peugeot.'

So then – though I knew he would never agree – I suggested that we take the train. He didn't even bother to reply. He has never set foot inside a train, nor an aeroplane – not even a lift . . . Whether or not he was afraid of them, who can tell?

In the end Ferrari decided on the Peugeot, even though Peppino had already prepared the Ferrari. As we were leaving, I asked what he thought of the 404. He said the brakes were poor but the rest was alright.

Ferrari said we would stop one kilometre short of the university and go the rest of the way on foot – a brilliant solution, typical of the diplomatic skills that were partly responsible for him going so far. He could be tough, he could shout, he could threaten, but what diplomacy he showed!

Between Maranello and Vignola, a country woman suddenly came out of a field on a bicycle. Ferrari made a masterful swerve to avoid her. If he had touched the brakes, he might not have done it. Always the great racing-driver.

The heat that day was unbearable. The kilometre walk – it may have been further – took its toll and we were quite breathless as we climbed the last flight of stairs. It was terribly sultry inside the ceremonial hall. There were a good many people present but, apart from myself, only one journalist, Athos Evangelisti.

When Ferrari came in, wearing his gown and mortar board and looking very imposing and severe, I was quite moved. The other person receiving a degree with him – a German professor of hydraulics – seemed to disappear by comparison.

To a hushed audience, Ferrari read a speech about the activities that had earned him the degree and which concerned mainly races and racing cars.

It was obvious that he was feeling emotional and when he reached the last sentence – 'to remember the young men whose yearning for achievement has even led them to make the final sacrifice. . .' – his eyes were red. Perhaps he was also remembering his father telling him to become an engineer when he had no desire to study. Perhaps he was remembering all the men who had died at the wheel of a racing car – any racing car, not just his own.

That evening, in a San Luca restaurant, Ferrari invited the professors and the Rector of the University – who was called Forni, if I remember rightly – to a dinner in celebration of his degree. He had brought with him a huge bottle of champagne, won by his drivers a few days before at the French Grand Prix. An event which at that time was almost always held at Reims, the champagne 'capital' of France. He went from one table to the next, smiling serenely, pouring out glasses of the delicious Veuve Cliquot-Ponsardin himself.

We returned to Modena and to the *Scuderia* [Italian for 'Stable']. There, we went into his office. On the desk was a small parcel. Ferrari opened it and found a small gold pillbox: a present from me, in honour of his degree. He looked at me and just said: 'Thank you . . . but why?'

A few days later, I received a note: 'Dear Gino, Many thanks for kindly accompanying me. However, I must courteously reproach you for your consideration. I do not know how to respond when faced with 'objects', even if they are examined in your presence, and neither can a letter express what I have experienced. I have a very curious way of accepting gifts. Now I shall have to settle my debts. I shall do this in a noisy way, not quietly like you. I cannot imitate you in these matters because – unfortunately – I have too tough a skin. Feelings take hold of me afterwards and perhaps too late. See you soon. Kind regards. Ferrari.'

The note was of course written in that violet ink. I had never asked Ferrari why he used it. Perhaps he wanted to distinguish himself even in his choice of ink?

But who is this Ferrari, this man who shouted, cursed and threatened, yet could not decide which car to use to go to Bologna for his degree? Who was this Ferrari who was so hard, unfriendly, imperious and so proud that he remained in his domain at Modena and Maranello and awaited the homage of the rest of the world?

He was above all a man who managed to do what he wanted, to achieve what he had dreamed of for years. In the words of Dario Zanasi, the journalist and man of letters, who worked for years on *Resto del Carlino* and was a sincere friend to Ferrari, he was: malicious, witty, subtly argumentative, hostile or friendly depending on the moment, stubborn, with unyielding courage and an almost prophetic spirit.

'During the war, in 1944 – a year that was so discouraging as to kill any vestige of hope in his struggle to save his workshop from plunderers and bombs – he said to me: "If I save anything, if they don't take everything away from me, then I am absolutely certain that the moment will come when I will be able to devote myself exclusively to the manufacture of racing cars and I will be able to see them racing every Sunday simultaneously in two or three different places around the world. Two or three wins in one day – don't you think that's a good plan?"'

Ferrari's 'almost prophetic spirit' had been proved right. In 1960, when they were awarding him an honorary degree in engineering, he had already won everything there was to win, apart from the Indianapolis 500 Mile Race. Gianni Brera wrote: 'And who, pray, is the greatest Italian today? I for my part am quite certain: Enzo Ferrari, the Stradivari of the motor-racing world.'

The Stradivari of the motor-racing world said one day: 'Engines are like sons: one settles down and studies and another signs cheques and is dissolute.' And again: 'Engines have a soul.' Harry Winston, who is considered the greatest dealer in precious stones in the world, used to say: 'Diamonds are like our sons. However many faults they may have, they belong to us and we cannot help loving them. Once you have them, you cannot give them up.' A peculiar parallel between two men, Ferrari and Winston, both of them sellers of jewels.

When I turned up at Modena in January 1956 with a team from television news for a report on the Bardhal-Ferrari which was to take part in the Indianapolis 500 Mile Race driven by Nino Farina, the great and courageous driver, ex-world champion and nephew of Pinin Farina, Ferrari suddenly asked me: 'Did you come with the six-legged dog?' [The six-legged dog is the logo of AGIP].

I didn't understand, so he explained: 'Since RAI [Italian broadcasting corporation] is part of IRI [institute for industrial reconstruction], you must have been using petrol provided by the State.' Now I saw what he meant. He must obviously have tried to link up with ENI [national hydrocarbons corporation] and therefore with AGIP [Italian general petrol company], but Mattei must have turned him down. It was pure conjecture on my part, but the tone used by the Commendatore suggested that anything to do with ENI rankled with him.

Then his show began – and what a great and incomparable actor he was. He took a sheet of paper and a red biro – he only used the fountain pen and violet ink for personal correspondence – and proceeded to draw me the Indianapolis 'basin'. I still have that sheet of paper and I wrote down everything that Ferrari rattled off to me: '6-cylinder Ferrari engine, 3 special Weber carburettors, bore 102mm, piston stroke 90mm, cylinder capacity 4420cc, 382 horsepower at 5800-6000 revs, engine weight 212kg. Probable speed 300kph, Indianapolis allows maximum speed of about 240, good instantaneous acceleration at high speeds of between 180 and 240, engine speed varies by about 1200 revs, 2 gears, consumption 30 litres per 100km, capacity of petrol tank 186 litres, oil tank 24 litres, fuel avgas 114/130 octane.'

I was taken aback, but in time I would understand that Ferrari, a man with an extraordinary memory, knew how to prepare himself thoroughly and punctually for interviews. The single-seater for Indianapolis had been assembled at San Lazzaro di Savena, on the outskirts of Bologna by the Maserati brother's company OSCA; Ferrari only sold the motor to Bardhal. But the venture did not get far and Nino Farina, if I remember rightly, did not manage to qualify.

That day marked the start of a constant relationship with Enzo Ferrari, who won my devotion.

Who was this Ferrari, this man whose fits of temper were so feared, who submitted to no will apart from his own, who immediately welcomed me as a friend and treated me almost as one of the family?

I began to study him, to learn all about him by running through all the newspaper cuttings and other recorded episodes that gradually revealed his story to me.

2

Tears in the Valentino park

Enzo Anselmo Ferrari was born at Modena on the 18 February 1898. Also born in that year were: Bertold Brecht, Alvar Aalto, Federico Garcia Lorca, Giuseppe Saragat, the great Neapolitan actor Toto, the great Russian film director Sergei Eisenstein, the writer and journalist Curzio Malaparte, the Russian biologist Trofim Denisovich Lysenko, Enrico Teodoro Pigozzi the founder of the French motorcar firm Simca, Willy Messerschmidt the famous aeronautical engineer and many other celebrities. It was a year of prodigies. Because of heavy snowfall which prevented his father from reaching the town hall, little Enzo was not registered until the 20th February and this was to be the official date of his birth.

He was an original from birth, and originality of behaviour and of judgement were to be his most important characteristics in his dealings with both people and events.

Ferrari wrote: 'In my adolescence, I had three main passions, three great dreams: to be an operatic tenor, to be a sports journalist and to be a racing-driver. The first dream evaporated through lack of voice and ear, the second persisted but in a diluted form and the third took its course and developed.' Ferrari did not become a journalist but he certainly showed that he could write. He was both a skilful talker and an able writer.

In December 1976, the *Gazzetta dello Sport* published a report by Enzo Ferrari which had appeared in that paper on the 16 November 1914, when he was not yet seventeen years old. Here it is: 'International 7 – Modena 1. The certainty of defeat and the lack of excellent players persuaded the Modena selectors to try a new formation that was both strange and incomprehensible. Suffice it to say that today the good Roberts was playing centre forward and none other than Molinari, the ex-captain, was called upon to substitute him as centre half. The two wing positions were taken by a reserve and by a player whose name has already been forgotten. It is easy to imagine the effectiveness or otherwise of the squad which today tried to oppose the virtuosos in black and blue. However, the Milan defence was put under pressure at times and had to fend off several corners, one of which allowed Modena to redeem its honour. Milan, who had excellent technique and great determination, appeared insecure in their defence, where Maggi was substituting Bavastro next to Fossati. The first-half goals were scored by Agradi in the 8th minute and by Aebi in the 15th, 20th and 36th minutes. In the second half, Cevenini III scored in the 12th minute from a penalty, Agradi in the 17th and Cevenini in the 23rd. Modena scored at the end of the match from a melée following a corner. Resegotti's refereeing was admirable in all respects. Enzo Ferrari.'

The *Gazzetta* commented: 'This short text, whose succinctness is exemplary, revealed the character of the man – precise in his observations and already able to argue convincingly while still only adolescent.'

Anyone who knows Ferrari would not find this report surprising. It should be emphasized that being able to write in this way in 1914 at the age of 16 was very significant, but the person who would one day become the King of Maranello could have done exceedingly well in any field. In my opinion, he would also have made a good Treasury minister and a wonderful administrator of great riches.

Whenever the piece written for the *Gazzetta dello Sport* was mentioned to him, his pride in it was obvious. He would smile cunningly and say: 'Could I get retrospective rights for it? Hmm, you never know . . .' He was attentive and precise and was always able to find just the right adjective. Behind his desk were a good number of dictionaries of the Italian language. One evening, when we were discussing a possible position to be adopted, I said: 'As an hypothesis, it's not bad.' He looked at me with those apparently inattentive eyes and reprimanded me: 'Hypothesis? Now Gino's making up words.' Then he took a dictionary and found the word 'hypothesis'. Months later, he used the same word in a conversation and added: 'You see, I can learn too.'

His attitude to me was strange. Sometimes he would speak to me formally and sometimes intimately. When he wrote, he always used the formal forms. Beppe Viola, a fellow broadcaster, once asked him the reason for this double treatment, but he never got a reply. A possible explanation occurs to me: if he always communicated with me in an intimate manner, he would perhaps be rewarding me too much?

When Enzo Ferrari was ten years old, his father, who owned a metalwork shop, took him to Bologna to see a motor race, where he was able to admire his idols, Vincenzo Lancia and Felice Nazzaro. He later said that it was on this day that he decided to take up racing, but did not seem to be very convinced of his statement.

In 1917 he enlisted in the army and then fell ill.

He recalled: 'I enlisted as a soldier in 1917 and was assigned to the 3rd Mountain Artillery, in the Val Seriana detachment, because in Italy at that time you were recruited according to your age, not your technical abilities. My knowledge of mechanics persuaded a Piedmontese sublieutenant to assign me to the blacksmith, to the section that made shoes for the mules. Then a serious illness meant that I was transferred to Brescia hospital and then to the Barracano in Bologna. I lay in that Bolognese hospital, consisting of dilapidated wooden huts, in a state of utter helplessness. Two operations and a great deal of treatment enabled me gradually to resume my work – with little means at my disposal and without any real experience, but with a great thirst for success.'

Ferrari overcame his misfortunes. He abandoned his 'state of utter helplessness' and grew strong. His later years would show just how strong a constitution he had.

At the end of the war, he approached Fiat with a letter of recommendation from his colonel. They turned him down. He wrote: 'It was the winter of 1918–1919 – a very hard winter and a painful memory for me. I found myself on the streets, the clothes on my back were freezing. I crossed the Valentino park, brushed the snow from a bench and flopped on to it. I was alone, my father and my brother Alfredo were no more. I was overcome by depression, and I wept. Many years later, in 1947, when Sommer had just won the Turin Grand Prix in the 12-cylinder Ferrari, I returned to sit on that same bench. The tears I shed that day had quite a different flavour.' Ferrari tells us just this much, but anyone who knows him can easily imagine his state of mind in the Valentino park after the win. He had a rare ability of knowing how to wait for his revenge and how to be a formidable opponent.

When he stood up from the bench in the Valentino park that first time, having been rejected by Fiat, the tears on his face had already dried. Ferrari was a young lion with claws of steel. He left in top gear, with his head down – but he did not leave Turin. The city owed him something. He found work in the Via Ormea in a light truck works; he had to test the trucks and take them to Milan, where the bodywork was built.

He paid careful attention to anyone who knew more than he did, and did not miss an opportunity to absorb the secrets of the trade. He had no time to spare for amusements and shows. All wrapped up as he was in his great adventure, from time to time he sent hurried, but reassuring, notes to his anxious mother in Modena. The robust young man was not content with getting to know the motor vehicle in all its aspects – he also wanted to race. Ten years had passed since the day his father took him to Bologna to see his first race, but his passion for it was still just as strong. In the streets of Turin, a youth with his cap on back-to-front and wearing goggles, would be seen driving various vehicles at great speed and with considerable skill. For the moment, all these vehicles were useful – they helped him to get his hand in, to get to know the soul of an engine, to understand the demands and dangers of the motor-racing trade. In Milan he met Ugo Sivocci, who had first been a cyclist and had then become a champion behind the steering wheel. Sivocci – who would be killed in a practice accident at Monza in 1923 – arranged for him to come to CMN [Italian abbreviation for 'national mechanical construction'] car factory in Milan, first as a tester, then as a driver. Ferrari lost no time.

Not so many months after the tears in the Valentino, he was thus racing in the Parma-Poggio di Bercetto in 1919, a classic hillclimb race. He came in fourth in his class in a 3-litre CMN. Then he went to the Targa Florio and came in ninth, after many ups and downs, including being stopped by the police because Vittorio Emanuele Orlando was finishing a speech and his audience was blocking the road!

In 1920, Ferrari also raced in an Isotta Fraschini Grand Prix 4500. The CMN was now proving inadequate to satisfy his dreams.

On the 24 October, he was driving an Alfa 4500 at the Targa Florio; he came in second. After the race, he moved to the Alfa

Romeo factory at Portello. 1921 produced a succession of victories, including a win in a 4500cc Alfa at the Aosta-Gran San Bernardo hillclimb.

Many years later, at Monza, during the trials of a Ferrari car, Pininfarina shared a table with me. I have always been surprised by the very great respect which the famous stylist showed Ferrari. It was almost as if he was in the presence of royalty, though Ferrari never did anything to impose himself on his friend. When we were talking about races and sportsmen of the past, Pininfarina very shyly said to me: 'And yet I had one great satisfaction. At one of the Aosta-Gran San Bernardo races, I came in before Ferrari, I beat him.' This must have been that same 1921 hillclimb.

More victories came, including success at the Circuito del Savio at Ravenna. Ferrari wrote: 'After the race, I met Count Enrico Baracca, father of the war hero. As a result of this, I later met the mother, the Countess Paolina and one day she said to me: "Ferrari, put my son's prancing horse on your cars. It will bring you luck." I still have a photograph of Baracca, with a dedication from his parents, granting me the emblem. The little horse was black and has remained so; I added the canary yellow background because it is the colour of Modena'.

Along with other animals like Jaguar's jaguar, Peugeot's lion, Porsche's filly and Lamborghini's bull, this little horse was to become one of the best known emblems in the world.

But Ferrari was already convinced – remember this prophetic spirit – that he was limited as a driver. He had too great a respect for the cars that were entrusted to him and perhaps he was not foolhardy enough. He had been resolved for some time to do something besides racing. In order to be able to do something else, he insisted on being given the task of finding engineers for the Alfa Romeo factory in Milan. He wrote: 'I began to think about relieving Fiat of some of its young technicians.' In this way, Luigi Bazzi made the trip from Turin to Milan. This was the faithful Bazzi who was to devote his skills to Ferrari throughout his entire life – and he was only the first. Bazzi told Ferrari that he should also 'relieve' Fiat of Vittorio Jano (who would later become one of the great car designers). So Ferrari went to Turin to attempt a 'peaceful robbery'. This was September 1923.

Years later, Jano, who always showed me great consideration, told me: 'I met this tall and bulky young man with a cap on his head. He immediately told me who he was and what he wanted. He was so persuasive and so precise that, even if my wife didn't want to move to Milan, I said yes.' Ferrari the 'siren', the great charmer, was successful even off the racing track. Later, in 1963, he would be surprised when Ferruccio Lamborghini, who was creating his motor company, took some of his own and some of Maserati's and Abarth's technicians. Perhaps he thought there was one rule for him and another for everyone else?

Ferrari only mentioned Lamborghini to me once – in the summer of 1962, I think. I remembered the meeting in *Il Giorno* on the 25th July 1972: 'One summer evening many years ago, I was dining with Enzo Ferrari. We talked about this, and that, and he said to me: "Do you know who came to see me today? That person who makes tractors near Modena. What's his name? You know . . ." He knew too but, as usual, he didn't want to attach any importance to it. I also knew, but I didn't say anything. Ferrari continued: "Never mind his name, it'll come to us. But he's a fine one. He told me that my cars – he has one – run the most smoothly of all. He accelerates to 200kph on the motorway, puts the car into neutral, then counts the kilometres he can coast: mine ran the farthest. Very nice of him." Ferruccio Lamborghini from Cento only ever spoke to Ferrari on that afternoon. He never saw him afterwards. One day he confided to me that he was afraid of the Commendatore. He was afraid because he had taken technicians and mechanics from him, as well as from Maserati, Abarth and other manufacturers. He took them because he had got the idea in his head to make cars. There was a very simple reason for this. He had owned examples of all the world's cars, but none of them, whatever it cost, had satisfied him. One got too warm ("when I had a girl with me, her mascara soon started running down her face"), another was too noisy, this one didn't brake, that one was uncomfortable.'

That is what I wrote in *Il Giorno*.

Today Ferruccio Lamborghini lives far away from cars and grows vines on Lake Trasimeno, from which he makes good wine. Dear Ferruccio, who spent ten years of his life on girls and managed to frighten Ferrari and Maserati. A man of little culture, extremely cunning, generous where necessary, and an Emilian through-and-through, like Ferrari. Extraordinary.

Jano set to work immediately and created the legendary Alfa Romeo P2 which, on its first appearance on the Circuito di

Cremona in 1924, won, covering the ten kilometres at almost 200kph. Luigi Bazzi, who wanted to hear the 'throb of the monster' from close to, was the riding mechanic to Antonio Ascari. Also in 1924, Alfa entered the French Grand Prix with Ascari, Campari, Wagner and Ferrari. The latter wrote that, because of ill-health, he was not present, but there is a photograph, taken at Lyon, of him at the wheel of the P2 with Bazzi by his side. Something must have happened between the trials and the race, but I don't know what. Some have maintained that he was afraid of the speed of the P2 . . .

Because of ill health, Ferrari reduced his sporting activity. The French Grand Prix put an end to racing for Fiat: defeated by Alfa, the Turin factory gave up.

No doubt the exodus of its technicians to Milan played some part in this decision. But was not the exodus provoked by Ferrari? The tears in Valentino park were thus avenged. Anyone who knew Ferrari will understand his state of mind on that day. His inner strength grew from the incident in Valentino park. What happened to Fiat, who had once turned him away, would happen to others . . .

On the 26th July 1925, Antonio Ascari was killed during the French Grand Prix at Montlhéry. A great friend disappeared forever in an aura of legend. Ferrari was stunned and many years later he would pour his affection on Antonio's son, Alberto, who was to become a great driver himself.

In 1927, Ferrari won the Circuito di Modena in an Alfa 1500 and did the same again a year later. These wins are also acts of revenge since neither then, nor at any other time, did 'his' city love him. Nor did he love it, and did little to improve relations with it. Races became ever rarer. In 1931 he won another classic hillclimb, the Bobbio-Passo del Penice. This was his last race, and his last victory. He drove an Alfa 2300 8-cylinder.

In 1932 Ferrari gave up the role of racing-driver. That year saw the birth of his son Dino, an event which obliged him to call a halt to the dangers of competition.

3

From racing-driver to leader of Scuderia Ferrari

Enzo Ferrari had already set out on the road that would take him far and turn him into The Great Ferrari. His personality had now completely matured and his skills, which had been developed by direct experience of races and men, were considerable. A first-rate organizer who issued reasoned and considered instructions, Enzo Ferrari had his own precise place in the world of motor-racing.

At the end of 1929, he founded the Scuderia Ferrari (he had wanted to call it 'Mutina' from the Latin name for Modena) with some associates who had money but who pulled out fairly soon. In 1932, the Scuderia took over management of Alfa Romeo in racing.

What was the Scuderia like? In Ferrari's words: 'it is a detached section of devoted Alfa customers who share technical and financial interests as well as an interest in racing.' The Scuderia, which was based in the viale Trento e Trieste (where the customer workshop is today) took mechanical components and cars from Alfa and modified and improved them. In practice, it was the racing subsidiary of the Milan firm, as Autodelta is today. The Scuderia got its customers to race – they were young, some of them very rich, and all of them had a passion for racing – so that it had a team, whose greatest members were Nuvolari, Varzi, Arcangeli, Campari, Borzacchini, Fagioli and Chiron. It also created other drivers, such as Brivio, Moll, Tadini, Trossi and Pintacuda.

The Scuderia also had its own publication which followed events and appeared at variable intervals. This venture into publishing was another 'necessity' for Ferrari. How many times have I heard him say that he wanted to start a paper, to enter the publishing world with something of his own? But he never did anything about it, perhaps because he was worried by how much such an enterprise would cost.

When he parted company with Alfa, he said that he felt like Vincenzo Lancia who had left Fiat in 1906 to set up on his own and become an independent and talented manufacturer.

When he started his Scuderia, Ferrari refined and improved his skills. He put down solid foundations that would one day allow him to become rich and famous. He worked, he provided fast cars to his drivers and customers and required them to pay him appropriately. If anyone could not afford a Ferrari Alfa, then he would have to do without; Ferrari did not give presents to anyone.

Activity at the Scuderia Ferrari would be intense for many years. It was thrown into competition with the world's manufacturers, and in particular with the cars produced by Auto-Union and Mercedes. Many 'miracles' were achieved with the help of the Scuderia's great drivers.

However, the German silver single-seaters, which had received generous help from Hitler, were just too good to be beaten.

Auto Union, which was created in 1932 by a fusion between Audi, Horch, Wanderer and DKW, profited from the genius of Ferdinand Porsche, who had also designed Mercedes racing cars in the late twenties.

The Auto Union of the time was a revolutionary car: rear engined with 16-cylinders and innumerable technical innovations in keeping with Porsche's philosophy of advanced design. The two German makes thus had very efficient creations at their disposal, which would allow even mediocre drivers to win – but Italian aces such as Varzi, Nuvolari and Fagioli were racing under German colours.

Alfa Romeo and Maserati tried everything and performed wonders, but the period 1934-39 belonged to the German cars.

1930 saw the Scuderia Ferrari's racing debut. In the meantime, the German industry was making its first appearances: Mercedes entered a 6000cc car with Caracciola-Werner in the Mille Miglia ['Thousand Mile' road race]. However, the race was won by Nuvolari and Guidotti (my dear friend and a remarkable racing 'archivist', an excellent driver, a great test-driver, who has always maintained that you win in the home stretch, where engine power is of paramount importance), who were the first to achieve an average speed of over 100kph in the Brescian race (100.45kph to be precise) and beat the Germans by more than an hour. The winning pair crossed the finishing line in a supercharged 1750. But Vittorio Jano, who was always quiet and serious, lost no time in preparing the supercharged 2300 with 8-cylinder in-line engine, which, designated as the 8C2300, would dominate sports car racing for years to come.

Among the Italian drivers who most distinguished themselves against the Germans was Tazio Nuvolari, who enjoyed the nicknames invented for him: 'Nivola,' 'The Flying Mantuan' ('mantovano volante'), 'The Red Devil'. He started his career as a motor cyclist and came late to the motor car, when he was over thirty. But he never tired of telling people that what he had done on two wheels could well be disregarded. In car-racing, Tazio, who was born in Castel d'Ario in 1892, was once again faced by his old motor cycle racing adversary, Archille Varzi from Galliate, who was twelve years younger. Their duels, both on the road and on the racing track, were memorable and they gave Ferrari the possibility of winning and of thus establishing his name.

Each race entered by Nuvolari was a test of courage and each race entered by Varzi was a test of logic at 200kph. There was a meeting between two worlds, between two approaches to motor-racing. Italy divided into two camps: the Nuvolari supporters and the Varzi supporters.

In 1935, Nuvolari provided the history of motor-racing with two memorable feats: the record for the flying kilometre and victory in the German Grand Prix. He won the record in the original *Bimotore* [twin-engined] Alfa conceived by Bazzi. The engines, one in front and one behind, were the Alfa Romeo type B, 2905cc, each capable of 270 horsepower at 5500rpm. The overall engine capacity of the car was therefore 5810cc and the actual power 540 horsepower. The 'red bolide' weighed 1000kg empty and it had a three-speed gearbox.

For comparison, recent Formula 1 Ferraris have had a 12-cylinder engine with a capacity of 3000cc and power outputs of more than 520 horsepower. Modern single-seaters weigh 600kg and have a five-speed gearbox (some makes even have six-speed gearboxes) and reach speeds of up to 300kph. Compared with pre-war racing cars, modern cars boast greater manoeuvrability, better braking and a ventilated interior. The effort required of the driver is certainly less than that of forty years ago.

Back to 1935. The testing of the Bimotore was carried out on the motorway between Florence and the sea at Altopascio – the original home of restaurateurs who became famous in Milan. Nuvolari did the flying kilometre at 321.428kph and the mile at 323.175kph. In the last 304.5 metres, the 'Flying Mantuan' reached 364.183kph, which means he was doing more than 100 metres per second. Bazzi told me that Nuvolari gave him 10,000 lire for that result, saying that 'the twin-engine drives like a Lancia Aprilia.' In other words the Bimotore was as well-mannered as a family car.

The second memorable exploit of 1935 occurred at the Nürburgring. Nuvolari's Alfa Romeo was certainly not in the same league as the silver Mercedes and Auto Unions (nine of them were in the race), but he managed to keep in Caracciola's wake in the fog, and then to win, causing Hitler's representative, who was supposed to award the prize to the winner, to hurry off!

To give an idea of what Nuvolari was like, here is the opinion of Nello Ugolini, who was known in racing circles as the *'maestro'* and who, having been with Alfa before the war, later held the position of racing manager for Ferrari and Maserati:

'In the first practices, our cars weren't doing very well, or rather, the Germans were going strong. On the Saturday morning, Tazio asked me if he could try Brivio's single-seater. He always used to let the others choose first, taking the car that was left. Anyway, he drove off and made the best lap time. Everyone was astonished. But if Nuvolari has a hand in it, anything is possible.

'On the morning of the race,' continued Ugolini, 'just before the start, Nuvolari told me to get a new Italian flag, because the one he had seen on the flagpole was old and faded. Since he was going to win, he told me, he wanted a colourful flag to be fluttering after the race. I agreed to get one, though I knew it would be difficult, if not impossible. However, I managed to find a new tricolour. Tazio's incredible effort and intelligence won him the race. When he got back to the pit, he held us back and said to me: "What about the flag?" I pointed it out to him and he smiled and said: "Now you can embrace me." That was Nuvolari.'

In 1936, Nuvolari and the Scuderia Ferrari went to the United States for the Vanderbilt Cup, which was held on a beaten earth course next to Roosevelt Field airport on Long Island. Apart from the European drivers, the best Americans – the men from Indianapolis – were of course also in the race. But Nuvolari won in his 12-cylinder Alfa Romeo, a good 12 minutes in front of the Frenchman Jean-Pierre Wimille, who was driving a 4900cc Bugatti.

Tazio won a silver cup, in which he could quite easily have sat, and the sum of 32,000 dollars. Giovanni Canestrini, a friend and incomparable expert for many of us automobile journalists, tells us in his *Una vita per le corse* ['A life devoted to racing']: 'When George Vanderbilt gave him the envelope with the cheque in it, Nuvolari took it and, without showing any emotion, put it casually into his pocket. Then he shook Vanderbilt's hand and went back to his seat. "Why doesn't he make sure the cheque's inside the envelope?" exclaimed Duray, the famous driver, probably reflecting the surprise of the invited crowd, who had thought they would witness an outburst of joy and emotion from the little Italian who had just won 32,000 dollars. A little later, the little Italian flatly rejected an offer of 5,000 dollars to speak for three minutes on the radio and refused contracts and tempting offers from advertisers. There was only one person he did not reject. A poor Italian living in America had implored him to take part in a race on a dirt track near New York. "If you come, you'll save me – I told them you would – please do me this favour." Nuvolari went. They gave him some sort of car, he did a few laps and then went home. He didn't care if he cut a poor figure among those unknown racing-drivers – all that mattered was that he had performed a good action.'

Refusing money – perhaps the drivers of today might learn something from this. That was what Nuvolari was like. It is a pity that little is known about his relationship with Enzo Ferrari.

Both men knew their own capabilities and both took their own work and their own rights seriously. Ferrari was always to hold Nuvolari close to his heart, and described him as 'matchless'. He once told me that though the two of them always spoke informally together, Nuvolari never called him by his first name, always just 'Ferrari'. About fifteen years ago, Ferrari said of him: 'As far as I'm concerned, there has been only one truly great racing-driver – Nuvolari. There is always a perfect balance between a car and its driver – 50 per cent car and 50 per cent driver. With Nuvolari, this relationship was completely overturned – he contributed at least 75 per cent of the total. Nuvolari's one great weapon was his courage, but he was also astute.

The memory of this great driver always influenced Ferrari's judgement of his drivers. The search for a new Nuvolari obsessed him and sometimes he thought he was close to one. Even Vittorio Jano, who was always so severe, had the highest esteem for Nuvolari. He affectionately called him the 'lad' and he told me more than once: 'It's not true that the lad used to break everything and come in with his car in pieces. Not at all. Almost always, all that was needed was to check the oil and water and the car was ready for another race. It was others, those who were supposed to be drivers with a knowledge of mechanics, who broke things, who asked too much of their cars and brought them back damaged.' Who 'those' drivers were, I never asked Jano. I think, though I may be wrong, that he was referring to Varzi . . .

In 1937, the Italians returned to the Vanderbilt Cup. Nuvolari was at the wheel of a 12-cylinder, 4000cc Alfa. He was among the leaders, along with Caracciola, Rosemeyer, Mays and Seaman, when his car caught fire.

Surrounded by flames, the great driver steered his car to the side of the track, to prevent danger to other cars, and then leapt from the cockpit. Rosemeyer won the race in the 16-cylinder, 6000cc Auto Union.

4

From Milan back to the home town

I n 1937 there was another important event, a turning-point in the Ferrari story. The 158, a car conceived by Ferrari and designed by Gioacchino Colombo, was created with the collaboration of Bazzi, Massimino, Nasi and Giberti. These were the names which Ferrari remembered. The new single-seater had a 1500cc supercharged engine and Ferrari immediately made four of them.

Remembering the 158 and the time leading up to its creation, Ferrari says: 'They were times of very complex work. I was trying above all to get to know the men and the business: drivers, organizers, managers, etc – but with no precisely defined responsibility. In that period, I also had the opportunity of synchronizing commercial activity as director of the Alfa Romeo branch office for Emilia, Romagna and the Marches, living alternatively at Milan and Bologna and at the same time managing not to abandon Modena completely. It was at this time that the idea of creating a racing-car completely of my own reached its maturity. Thus the 158 Alfa came into being in Modena. This was the car which would be called the Alfetta after the war and which would allow the Milan company to win two world championships.

The following year, Ferrari ceded everything to Alfa, liquidated the original Scuderia Ferrari and was taken on as director of Alfa-Corse [the motor racing division of Alfa Romeo], committing himself to staying away from racing and racing-cars in an independent capacity for at least four years. In his own account, which is the guiding thread for our treatment of this period, Ferrari tells us he was earning 540,000 lire a year. Not bad!

The new organization made use of Luigi Bazzi as head of the car manufacturing department, Scapinelli for the administrative section and Nello Ugolini for the organization of races.

Alfa Romeo's racing 'customers' continued to have their cars prepared and to obtain assistance for their races at the building in Modena, which had been the headquarters of the original Scuderia Ferrari and where the necessary specialized personnel were retained for the Scuderia's new role.

The Scuderia would remain Ferrari's centre of activity for years. It was a long, low building with a ground floor and a first floor (where his family lived), containing small, modest offices with mass-produced furniture and with photographs of races and racing-drivers on the walls. It was in these rooms that customers and drivers waited to see the Commendatore. His office was fairly big. There were numerous photographs reminding him of his great adventures and on a shelf next to his desk were portraits of dead drivers, and a great quantity of cups and trophies. Around the courtyard were workshops and a showroom – which was modest and badly lit – for cars that were to be dispatched to the wealthy people who had ordered them.

Today, the Scuderia is just the same as all those years ago. It has been tended and painted more frequently, but the space has remained as it was. It is now used for repairs to customers' cars and for the delivery of new cars.

However, Ferrari's position with the Milan firm was a burden to him and in 1939 he left Alfa. He saw himself as a motivator of men and a solver of technical problems. He had never considered himself to be a designer or inventor, just an organizer. He was champing at the bit and wanted to set up on his own. He said: 'I do not want to give up my way of thinking. I'm keeping my bad habits and going back to my home town.' Later, he would write: 'By deciding to leave, I felt that I was making a promise to show those who favoured my departure that the twenty years spent in the firm could not be described as the usurpation of a position, but as a recognition of my talent and unbending loyalty. I left Alfa to show people there who I was – an ambitious project, enough to ruin a man!'

But not Ferrari, and the people at Alfa realized it later. Thus Ferrari returned to Modena feeling 'almost ferociously attached to my home town.'

He immediately founded *Auto Avio Costruzioni* [Auto-aviation construction]. He was alone and he remembered what his father often used to tell him: 'A company is perfect when the number of partners is uneven and less than three.' Many years later he would make less use of this rule, but by then he had changed and was desperately trying to arrange the continuation of his company.

Ferrari's first project in his new situation was to produce a racing-car for the 1940 Mille Miglia held on the fast Brescia-Cremona-Mantua-Brescia route. Since Ferrari could not give his name to the car, he called it '815', as it had an 8-cylinder engine with a capacity of 1500cc.

Some years later, the Maserati brothers too would find they were not able to give their name to the cars they made in Bologna. In 1947, the brothers, Bindo, Ettore and Ernesto completely abandoned the company to the Orsi family from Modena on condition that the brothers could no longer use the name Maserati. In this way, the *OSCA*, or *Officina Specializzata Costruzioni Automobili* [Specialized Automobile-Construction Workshop], came into being at San Lazzaro di Savena.

The 815 was an assembly of Fiat components and others made at the Auto Avio Costruzioni. The choice of Fiat parts was logical: they were easy to obtain and, more importantly, they provided an opportunity of avoiding Alfa Romeo parts. Ferrari was not a man to sink to such a level. The car's designer was Alberto Massimino, who had worked on the 158 several years before.

Two 815's were made and assigned to Alberto Ascari (this was the first meeting between the 22 year-old from Milan – who had already raced on motorbikes – and his father's great friend) and to Marquis Lotario Rangoni Macchiavelli from Modena. The 815's did not go far, but they showed that Ferrari had now started up on his own as an independent manufacturer.

Unfortunately both of these cars have disappeared without trace. I often asked Ferrari why he didn't keep these important cars, the ones that had given him the most satisfaction. He always told me that he could not allow himself such a luxury, because if you want to run a museum, you need money. But perhaps the real reason was different: once a car had stopped racing, he considered it a dead creature that could no longer do anything for him. Once the car had performed its function, it was to be destroyed, erased. Memories serve no purpose. The experience gained from a car remained on paper, on the drawing board. The physical image was perhaps only a homage to what it had once been and Ferrari had no use for romantic relics. What his cars had given him remained inside, in his heart and mind. At least, this is what I assume.

The race, at which I was an enthusiastic spectator on the Cremona bend between the roads to Brescia and Mantua, was won by a BMW driven by the German pair, Huscke von Hanstein and Baumer. The Baron von Hanstein, who was to be well-known in the motor-racing world after the war as Porsche's racing manager, wore overalls with the SS insignia on them.

When Ferrari was starting his memoirs he asked me whether it would be a good idea to publish the photograph showing von Hanstein after he won the Mille Miglia. I replied that I did not think so. He 'obeyed' me. Then, in the following editions, the photograph suddenly appeared. A typical example of Ferrari's attention to detail – nothing more.

It was not that he had anything against the Baron from Stuttgart, but the idea of showing him wearing the unpopular insignia appealed. In fact he had cordial relations with von Hanstein, both when the latter was racing manager for Porsche and when he joined the small group of men who ran the international sport of motor-racing.

In 1943, AAC moved to Maranello (leaving the Scuderia at Modena), a small town 17km from the city on trunk-road number 12 between Abetone and Brennero, at the foot of the Appenines. Just over 100 workers were employed, a large number of them women. Small 4-cylinder engines for training aircraft and petrol-driven grinding machines were made. There was no shortage of work, but it was an humiliation for Ferrari to have to produce 'objects' that were so different from cars.

He remembers: 'I moved to Maranello at the end of 1943 because of the industrial decentralization law which was imposed on factories. I had about forty workers at Modena and this number increased considerably in the course of the war, so that I could eventually count on 140-160 at Maranello. There were no shares in the new firm, it was private. Why Maranello? I chose this place at the foot of the so-called Gothic Line because I owned a piece of land in the immediate vicinity of the site of the present factory.'

This piece of land was then used for growing fruit, especially cherries, and now it is the site of the Fiorano track, which is famous throughout the world, being the highly sophisticated test site for Ferrari racing and GT cars.

Ferrari's account continues: 'The years that followed were very useful in terms of experience, although they were painful because there was obviously no room for motorcars. I started to work for the *Compagnia Nazionale Aeronautica* [National Aeronautic Company] in Rome, making small 4-cylinder engines for flying school aircraft used to train future pilots. Then one of my colleagues, Enrico Nardi, who would later also become a manufacturer, introduced me to an agreeable friend of his from Turin, Corrado Gatti. Gatti was a dealer in machine tools and asked me to make petrol-driven grinding machines of various types copied from German models. These machines were needed in particular for the manufacture of ball-bearings.

'I asked the Germans for a manufacturing licence, but they politely refused, explaining that they could not grant that sort of licence, since these machines were too complex and they – the Germans – were unable to offer adequate technical assistance for their production. However, my lawyer informed me that under then current Italian law I was able to reproduce these machines, since they had not been made in Italy, without committing any offence. So I set to work, humbly copying. The reproduction was so faithful that an important figure in one of the big national industries wrote to me saying: "The grinding-machines you have provided are just as effective as the originals."

'On the 8th September 1944, when the Germans arrived at the Ferrari workshop at Maranello to draw up an inventory, the commanding officer, an engineer who was well-known for his previous technical and business activities in Italy, paid me this compliment: "Signor Ferrari, I know that you make excellent German grinding machines and so all the ones you make will be requisitioned by us". Evidently the lack of manufacturing licence, of consultation and of technical drawings, had not prevented me from producing machines whose reputation had spread beyond the borders. The end of the war did not find me unprepared, despite the fact that my workshop had been bombed on the 4th November 1944 and again in the following February. I had continued to develop projects for racing cars and when the storm had passed I hurriedly got rid of the machine tools.'

The factory then consisted of some long and low hangars

arranged in a triangle and this remains the basic structure of Ferrari today. Where the GT cars used to be made, in the hangar on the left of the entrance, is now the racing department, independent of the rest of the factory. Behind the main body, large well-lit departments have recently appeared. These are intended for production and people who knew the old Ferrari works will be impressed by the sight of people working around long, well-lit assembly lines.

Order and cleanliness have always been characteristics, so much so that you might think the Ferrari works produced clocks, not motorcars. Ferrari's office was at the front of the first hangar. It was generally possible to see into it from the courtyard, since Ferrari never hid from his staff or from the curious. The walls were painted dark blue and the ceiling white. In front of the desk was a conference table with eight places. Behind the table was a television and on the wall a photograph of Dino with three plastic flowers in the colours of the Italian flag.

The ever-present diary lay on the desk along with some technical publications. On the left a low bookshelf with books, a clock, the crystal head of the rampant colt and immediately above, on the wall, was the famous portrait of Francesco Baracca in front of his aircraft.

Between the shelves and Ferrari's revolving chair was a small table with two telephones and a card-holder containing the telephone numbers most used by him. The card was inserted into a small apparatus and the number was dialed automatically.

Ferrari's first office at Maranello, which is near the present one, is now occupied by Gozzi, the press secretary. The desk is still the same – so big that in order to shake Ferrari's hand, you had to stretch over it. This was especially difficult for women. It was in this office that an American woman journalist, a good friend of Evangelisti and of myself, had been astonished both by the dimensions of the desk and what they involved, and by an episode that occurred during her visit.

After Ferrari had welcomed her and obliged her to stretch right over the desk to shake his hand, he showed her a letter he had received from some young Americans who told him that the music made by the engines in his cars was like that of the great European composers. There was a flow of other, similar, praise and Ferrari seemed to be enraptured by the letter's comment. However, it was summer and the office windows were open. Suddenly, a test-driver started up an engine in the courtyard. The walls of the office started to shake, so loud was the noise. Ferrari, who until a few moments ago had been so happy about the 'roar like a thumping symphony', called in his secretary and shouted to him: 'Shut the window, that noise is terrible and the lady and I can't hear each other.'

5

The first car called Ferrari

The war finished and Ferrari, who was 47 years old, set off at a great pace. He already had a head start because he had never completely abandoned racing cars and had been planning and trying out various ideas.

As if by magic, Gioacchino Colombo reappeared at Maranello – he too was looking for a new beginning. The skilful technician who had designed the 158, did not want to waste any time and set to work with Ferrari. Their dream was to build a 12-cylinder engine. Ferrari wrote: 'The 12-cylinder is an engine I have always longed for, ever since I saw the photographs of a 12-cylinder Packard that was racing at Indianapolis back in 1914. We talked and debated and finally we drew up a plan for the 12-cylinder engine that is still the flagship of Ferrari production.' Much later, in 1974, he added: 'Even the other national manufacturers and foreign technicians who laughed at the lineage of Ferrari engines have now crossed their technological Rubicon.' Ferrari could not resist the remark; his cutting comment was aimed not so much at BRM and Matra, but at Alfa Romeo who, having tried an 8-cylinder engine in their 33 sports-racing car, adopted a 12-cylinder one, and what is more a boxer like Ferrari's then flat-12. He always managed to make a reproach when he felt he had to. He might have to wait for years, but if he could, he would get satisfaction, no matter what the cost.

With regard to boxer engines, engines with horizontal cylinders facing one another (the main advantages are a lower centre of gravity and better balance: the best known cars that use this type of engine are the Porsche 911, Citroën 2CV, Volkswagen Beetle, Lancia Gamma, Alfasud and Citroën GS). Ferrari should have remembered that, in fact Alfa Romeo made a racing-car with a flat-12 engine before Ferrari, the 1500cc single-seater type 512 in 1939. In Alfa Romeo's museum at Arese, the 512 is described as the first racing car with a 12-cylinder horizontally opposed engine. The designer of the 512 was the Spanish technician Wilfredo Ricart, who had put Enzo Ferrari in a position where he had to leave Alfa. In his memoirs, Ferrari does not forget to describe Ricart as only he knows how: 'Ricart had straight, greasy hair. He dressed with a somewhat middle eastern style, in jackets that had long sleeves so that I could not see his hands. When he held out his right one to shake, it felt like a piece of dead meat. Our Spanish friend wore shoes with such thick rubber soles that one day I had to ask him why. With great seriousness, Ricart replied that it was a natural precaution to be taken by a technician. "The brain of a great technician should be carefully protected from the roughness of the ground." Troubled by such statements, I went on to suggest to Gobbato, the director of Alfa, that the Spaniard must no doubt be a very interesting person, destined for a superior calling, for great achievements, not for designing racing-cars. Gobbato criticized me severely – perhaps he interpreted my judgement of Ricart as an expression of envy. Unfortunately time proved me right. The first car of the new series produced some strange results when it was tested for the first time. When the steering wheel was turned to the right, the wheels moved to the left and as for the engine, it always categorically refused to allow its true sound to be heard, because the crankshaft would flex at the back. Another project was the 12-cylinder rear-engined 1500cc. When Ricart introduced it, it was with a communication which stated that the 158 was obsolete and good only for the scrapyard or the museum. This car also was never able to take part in a race. A 158 engine was later mounted on the chassis and, as cruel fate would have it, the great mechanic and test-driver Marinoni died in this car on the Milan-Varese motorway.

'The technician left Alfa Romeo another novelty – an unusual radial aviation engine. He presented part of the engine to Gobbato along with a diagram illustrating its great efficiency. I learnt from the faithful Bazzi of a strange omission in this, ie, the lack of any reference to the fact that the compressor – it was a supercharged engine – was driven by an auxiliary engine! My disagreement with Gobbato became aggravated. I was obliged to tell him that, as in the case of the 158 cars and the liquidation of the Scuderia Ferrari, I had not changed my way of thinking. He answered me with the following words: "I am the director at Alfa Romeo and I cannot disassociate myself from a colleague in whom I have put my trust. As for the advice you give me, Ferrari, I cannot accept every piece of it without reserve or at least without some discussion." I apologised, perhaps having deserved such a harsh reply, but added that it was not a question of discussing or unreservedly accepting what I said, just that I did not like the way that such ideas were accepted [from Ricart]. The rift thus became irreparable and led to my dismissal from Alfa.'

The fact that the 512 was not a racing-car was confirmed to me by Consalvo Sanesi, Alfa's main test-driver and a very brave man, who drove the car. Ferrari had given a severe, but legitimate judgement of the single-seater, about whose qualities Alfa had made certain unfounded claims. The truth should be told.

As the workshop was being repaired and rebuilt after the destruction caused by bombs, the first Ferrari, the '125', came into being. 125cc is the capacity of each cylinder: when multiplied by 12, it gives 1500cc.

The engine in the 125 S was a 60° V12, with a bore of 55mm, a piston stroke of 52.5mm and a total capacity of 1496.77cc. At 7000rpm and with a compression ratio of 8.5 to 1, it generated 100 horsepower. It was supplied by three Weber downdraft twin-choke carburettors and had coil ignition with two distributors, rear-wheel drive, gearbox in unit with the engine, five gears plus reverse and hydraulic drum brakes. The 125 S's wheelbase was 2.42 metres, the front track 1.255 metres and the rear track 1.2 metres. The weight was 750kg and the fuel tank capacity 75 litres. The car could reach 46kph in first gear, 64 in second, 103 in third, 142 in fourth and 153 in fifth – figures that seem modest by today's standards.

As a sports-racing car the 125 was not in any way revolutionary, but it did have a very powerful and robust engine. In fact it was a great engine. Ferrari himself once said: 'I build engines and attach wheels to them.' But when he found he was being left behind, particularly by the British manufacturers, he had partly to change his mind. In his own words: 'Perhaps a certain amount of underestimating occurred over the years. I have always attached much more importance to the engine than to the chassis and have endeavoured to achieve high rates of power and efficiency, in the conviction that this would contribute not just 50 but 80 per cent to the success in a race. And, in fact, this held true, and it remains true, if you have at least 30 horsepower more for the same capacity. But when competitors start to catch up both in terms of engine power and of road-holding ability, shortcomings in the chassis suddenly become more serious. This is due to the extreme demands that are now made of the vehicle. We are now convinced that no racing-car can last more than one season. It has to be continually modified if we want to maintain the rate of technical development. Progress which, in time, we hope to consolidate, with the help of the knowledge gained from the 139 prototype engines we have made since 1946.' This quotation dates from 1974. It took years for Ferrari to be convinced that the engine is not everything. But since he was such a skilful interpreter of other people's techniques, this realization came in time for him to recover – to recover and to overtake the British experts.

'In April 1947, the 125 was ready. It had passed all tests to the satisfaction of Ferrari and his men, and now a more delicate step had to be taken, that of entering it in a race . . . The venue was the Piacenza circuit on the 11th May. Two Ferrari 125s were entered – one to be driven by Franco Cortese, and the other by Nino Farina: considered to be Tazio Nuvolari's heir on account of his skill and daring. There were thirty laps to cover, making a total of 99km. In the end, only Cortese was able to take part in the race because Nino Farina went off the road in practice and damaged his car. Cortese, numbered 128, was in third place until the 21st lap. He then shot into the lead and stayed there until the 27th lap, at which point he was more than 24 seconds ahead of Angiolini's Maserati. Suddenly the engine cut out because the petrol pump was malfunctioning and he had to drop out of the race. However, the 125 had at least shown it was capable of putting up a good fight.

Ten years later, in 1957, I started to write the story of the Ferrari company. I began at the beginning of the century and described Ferrari the man, his life and the setting up of the company. Then the story finished in 1956 and I never took it any further. It started like this on: Monday 26th May, 1947, in *Tuttosport*, which then appeared every three weeks. Space as precious as paper. Headlines not too big, reports short and concise. On the fourth page in two columns:

'Franco Cortese's "Ferrari"
Fastest car in Roman Grand Prix'

'The news: The duel between the "Ferraris" and Barbieri's Maserati ended in victory for the former, thus removing any doubts raised by its recent debut at Piacenza. (Then came the results.)
Victory, the first victory, for a new Italian car. A new make – another example of Italian genius and hard work – joins the ranks of the older motor companies.
"The Ferrari has won", shout the motor-racing enthusiasts. This is news indeed.
'For the manufacturer and his workers the hour of victory is a signal for renewed effort and great sacrifice. Alone in his office, Enzo Ferrari looks straight ahead, into the infinity of the future. He sees many things the others do not know yet. When the car returns from victory it is already a dead thing to be dissected . . .'

At that time, we were allowed to make the mistake of writing 'Ferraris', but soon everyone learnt how to write the name Ferrari correctly.

In only its second race, the Ferrari had already won.

Only one 125 was present, driven by Franco Cortese, who beat all the other competitors. Cortese then won again at Vercelli in the Coppa Faini. The 14th Mille Miglia took place on the 21st and 22nd June, Cortese, together with Marchetti, covered 400km but withdrew at Fano because of damage to the cylinder-head gasket.

All this moved the great Nuvolari. He was now 55 years old and not in the best of health. He knew that nobody would be likely to entrust a car to him: but Ferrari had not forgotten the past and knew that if Nuvolari won a race in his car the victory would be worth twice as much. On the 6th July, the Mantuan racing-driver raced at Forli in the Coppa Luigi Arcangeli and won the under 1500cc sports category, achieving the fastest lap. The Ferrari-Nuvolari double-act had been recreated and both men felt rejuvenated. Tazio won a second victory in the first Circuito di

Parma, coming in ahead of Cortese in another 125.

A classic race was on the programme for Ferragosta [the Feast of the Assumption] – at the Circuito di Pescara on August 16th: twenty 25.5km laps, making a total of 510km. The 125 had been enlarged to two litres and was entrusted to Cortese once more. But, surprisingly, the race was won by that Cremonese of Neapolitan origin, Vincenzo Auricchio in the Fiat 1100 Stanguellini, with coachwork by Bertone. Auricchio became one of the most compelling racing-drivers in the world while he was at the wheel of that little 1100, but when he moved on to more powerful cars he failed to repeat his great feats. Auricchio won and in second place was Cortese, who did the fastest lap at an average of 126.807kph. On the 12th October, in the second Turin Grand Prix, the Frenchman Raymond Sommer won the 504km race. Sommer, in the Ferrari, also achieved the fastest lap at an average of 112.753kph.

For years, Ferrari would say that Sommer's win at the Valentino was the win that gave him the most pleasure. It was then that he went to the bench in the Valentino, the same bench he had sat on in the winter of 1918-1919, when Fiat had been unable to take him on. After so many years, Ferrari finally had his revenge in Turin, the very place where he had wept with despair. The win and the taste of revenge gave him renewed energy. The goals he had set himself became more obtainable.

In 1947, Ferraris took part in 14 races and achieved seven wins and four second places – not bad!

The winning Ferrari was the 166, the enlarged version of the 125. Ferrari prepared three versions of the 166: the Sport with a 1992cc engine developing 90 horsepower at 6000rpm, the Inter with 110 horsepower at 6500rpm and the Corsa with 130 horsepower at 7000rpm. The latter was the type that won at the Valentino. A leaflet from the factory said: 'The 166 Sport is a fast GT, the 166 Inter is for the international sports formula and the 166 Corsa for international formula 2.'

1948 started well. On the 4th April, the eighth *Giro di Sicilia* [Tour of Sicily] was held. This 1080km course was one of the most difficult. Clemente Biondetti, who was paired with 'Igor', was at the start in a 166 Sport. The great Florentine road-racer won with an average of 88.866kph. Biondetti was also to win prestigious victories for Ferrari, as he did in the past for Alfa Romeo. In 1948, he was once again the winner in the famous Mille Miglia, with the average achieved in 1938 – 135.391kph.

The first Ferrari bulletin came out. At the bottom, Enzo Ferrari wrote a piece entitled *'Return'*. 'After a long gap imposed on it by world events, the Scuderia Ferrari has returned to racing. The return has been fundamental and complete. It is no longer merely a sporting organization that enters races throughout the world, or prepares men and machines; it is above all a manufacturer of racing cars. This manufacturing activity, which began in 1938 with the 8-cylinder 1500cc 158, is now the main work carried out by Ferrari. The battle started in May last year and has continued with a series of onerous, often thankless experiences. The desired results have been achieved and are a just reward especially for those collaborators who have always calmly put their trust in us. Without any help, but believing in our cause, we have worked away – worked away with the obstinacy of country artisans. It may be difficult to achieve supremacy in the technical field, where there are no revolutions, just slow and steady developments, but it is even more difficult to hold on to it. With unity of purpose, we are working and we shall continue to work to maintain our position and to achieve further successes.'

'Strike while the iron is hot' is an old saying and Ferrari certainly knew how to strike. He reasserted the fact that the Alfa Romeo 158 came into being at Modena and was therefore one of his creations (they certainly wouldn't have agreed with this in Milan) and the fact that he had become a manufacturer. No mention of the pre-war Ferrari – that no longer mattered: here was another example of self-gratification, typical of the man who had the obstinacy of a country artisan. Ferrari was a man who took his revenge and always said what he thought: if it hurt his target, so much the better.

On the 2nd May 1948 the 15th Mille Miglia was held over a distance of 1829,988km, the longest ever. Giovanni Canestrini remembers: 'For its 12-cylinder car, the Maranello firm could count on Biondetti, who had already won the Targa Florio in the Giro di Sicilia, on its customers the Besana brothers, on Cortese and on Righetti. Nothing was said about Nuvolari and he himself had not expressed his wishes – he was waiting in the wings. It was known that Tazio, who was then living at Gardone, would be present at Brescia in order to take part in the tests. Suddenly, messengers were sent from Alfa Romeo in Milan to offer Nuvolari the wheel of one of two experimental cars. Ferrari, who, as ever, was well-informed and quick to act, shot from Maranello to Brescia, arriving before the messengers from the Milanese firm, and enlisted Nuvolari's support. Nuvolari, supported by Scapinelli, thus set off in a 12-cylinder, 2-litre Ferrari while Alfa Romeo were obliged to entrust such a demanding race to Sanesi and Sala. Thus the chivalrous and profitable rivalry between Alfa Romeo and Ferrari – which lasts to this day – continued to flourish.'

Canestrini did not have an easy character, but he knew how to be kind. Describing the rivalry that Ferrari felt towards Alfa as 'chivalrous and profitable' is indeed an act of kindness. By 'stealing' Nuvolari from Alfa, Ferrari was continuing his personal crusade and we can only guess at his satisfaction when he knew that he had arrived before the Milanese.

Canestrini continues: 'Alfa's attempt to enlist Nuvolari was also due to the fact that the presence of the Ferraris in that Mille Miglia was threatening to interrupt a series of wins started by Campari in 1928 and disturbed only once in 1931 by Caracciola's Mercedes. The race, which started at midnight on May 2nd, the weather being wet and windy, turned into a relentless duel between the two Ferrari standard-bearers, supported by Navone and Scapinelli respectively.

Before Padua, Tadini-Canavesi dropped out in their Alfa Romeo; between Forli and Rome it was the turn of Taruffi (Cisitalia) and Gurgo Salice (Alfa Romeo); between Rome and Livorno [Leghorn], Giannino and Paolo Marzotto (Aprilia), Sanesi and Sala (Alfa Romeo), Cortese-Marchetti and the Besana brothers (Ferrari) and the two Tasseras (Maserati) all withdrew; between Livorno and Firenze [Florence], Ascari-Bertocchi (Maserati) dropped out; between Bologna and Asti, it was Bonetto-Maritano (Cisitalia), Cornacchia-Facetti (Cisitalia) and Nuvolari-Scapinelli (Ferrari).

Biondetti arrived at Brescia with an average speed of 121.227kph, 28 minutes ahead of the little 1100 S driven by Comirato, who had his wife Lia by his side. Nuvolari had spared no effort in this race, which he hoped to win. Before Rome, he had gone off the road and lost a mudguard. At the control in the capital, he had also got rid of the bonnet, which could no longer be attached because the catch was broken, and had continued in the rain with an open engine compartment. A little after Livorno, a second spin on a bend at Montenero had damaged a spring and broken the fixings of the mechanic's seat, which became almost completely detached. Finally at Reggio Emilia, when he was hoping to be able to shoot victoriously over the finishing line (he had gone through Bologna with a 29 minute lead over Biondetti-Navone), Nuvolari had to give up after the complete collapse of a rear spring shackle pin which had been damaged during the spin at Montenero.

Poor, great, Nuvolari. A little after his retirement from the race, Ferrari said to him: 'Cheer up, Tazio, there's always next year.' Tazio replied: 'Ferrari, at our age, days like this do not often come again. Remember that and try to experience them to the full if you can.'

Ferrari held Nuvolari in great esteem. When Tazio's second son, Alberto, died, an even stronger respect bound Ferrari to the great driver. Nuvolari had lost two sons, both at 18 years of age – Giorgio in 1937 and Alberto in 1946. Ferrari had just one son, Dino, whose health had been bad for years, and he knew that he would die. This shared pain brought him very close to Tazio and, by giving him a racing car, he tried to alleviate Tazio's sorrow and make his life less bitter.

Biondetti's victory was clouded by Nuvolari's misfortune. But the Ferrari had inscribed its name on the roll of honour in the most prestigious long-distance race in the world. Of the 24 times the Mille Miglia was held, between 1927 and 1957, Alfa Romeo won 11 times, Ferrari eight, Mercedes twice and BMW, Lancia and OM once each. By winning the Mille Miglia, Ferrari joined the ranks of the great car makers. But, in 1957, this race was to give Ferrari one of his greatest causes for sorrow – the death of De Portago, his co-driver and ten spectators. The incident was followed by a trial which imposed conditions on the manufacturer for several years.

After the 1948 race, many said that if Nuvolari had been in a berlinetta like Biondetti, he would probably have won. But Nuvolari could no longer race shut inside a cabin. The year before, he had come in second in the small Cisitalia spider after a race which, as usual, was very exciting. His co-driver was Carena, who told me how, before the race, Cisitalia had offered the great Tazio the choice between two cars, a berlinetta and a spider. 'Nuvolari,' said Carena, 'wanted to try out both of them with me. Afterwards he said that the berlinetta would be more powerful and would avoid the problem of bad weather, but he couldn't breathe in it and so he had to choose the spider. In fact he almost fainted on the way to the start and threw himself out of the cockpit, hurting his hand. But he was incomparable and but for the trouble with the ignition, we would have won magnificently.'

Let us return to the 30th May 1948, when Ferrari achieved its first success abroad: Biondetti won the Stockholm Grand Prix, beating Cisitalia, Simca and Alfa Romeo. In September, Luigi Chinetti won the Paris 12 Hour Race in the 2000, with an average speed of 116.753kph. Two Ferraris took part in the Grand Prix at Monza – Sommer, who was unwell and withdrew in the 7th lap and Farina, who gave up in the 53rd. This race was important for Ferrari because it represented the debut of the single-seater car. The 125 sports car had become a Formula 1 machine – a supercharger had been added to its engine: the 1500cc unit now developing 230 horsepower at 7000rpm.

The Monza race on the 17 October 1948 was very important to Enzo Ferrari. The Alfa to beat was the 158, *his* 158, and a single-seater was needed to accomplish this task. The Formula 1 125 did not manage it but it was the first, uncertain step towards another great piece of revenge. Ferrari, though he did not know when this revenge would be won, knew how to wait for it and worked night and day.

On the Monthléry track on the 3rd November, the Ferrari 2000, with Chinetti at the wheel, broke the world speed record at 202.243kph and the international records over a distance of 200km (average speed 203.378kph) and over a distance of 100 miles (average speed 203.435kph). Wind and rain did not prevent Luigi Chinetti's great achievement.

In 1948, the little factory took part in 28 contests and had 10 wins, 11 second places and 6 thirds. A very impressive result.

The 1949 season started early. In February, the third Rosario Grand Prix was held in Argentina and was won by Farina in the Ferrari Formula 1, ahead of Maserati and Alfa Romeo. On the 21st May in Brussels, Gigi Villoresi was at the wheel of a Ferrari. It was his first appearance in a vehicle bearing the prancing horse and he performed magnificently by winning and by achieving the fastest lap. A few days later, the Milanese driver, who was a friend of Alberto Ascari, won again in Luxembourg in the only Ferrari present. On the 12th June, Ferrari achieved a real coup at the third Bari Grand Prix, where the 427km race was won by the Ascari's Ferrari Formula 2 car, which was followed over the line by all the other Ferraris driven by Cortese, Bonetto, Villoresi-Landi and Vallone.

Alberto Ascari was introduced to Ferrari by Felice Bonetto, who was among the bravest drivers of the post-war period. But Ferrari would have none of it and told Bonetto that he would not take on a driver who had destroyed his 815 in the 1940 Mille Miglia. He needed drivers who could win and who showed some respect for their car. Racing cars cost money. He also wrote a letter to Bonetto, reminding him that the 7000rpm limit was absolute – in the last races he had used up to 7200rpm and such liberties cost money.

The 1949 Mille Miglia missed out the stretches between Turin and Milan. The course was Brescia, Cremona, Livorno, Rome, Terni, Popoli, Pescara, Padova [Padua], Verona, Brescia. Ferrari were the favourites and were represented by three 2000s driven by Biondetti, Taruffi and Bonetto, and other cars driven by Besana, Cortese and Bracco. Bonetto-Carpani went into the lead. By the time they reached Rome, they had an average speed of over 132kph and were four minutes ahead of Taruffi and seven ahead of Biondetti. At Pescara, Taruffi was leading, followed eight minutes later by Biondetti, while Bonetto was having problems with his brakes. After Ravenna, Taruffi had to withdraw, Biondetti was leading, followed by the Alfa driven by Rol-Richiero, but Bonetto made a recovery and won back second place. Biondetti, who had raced with Salani, won, with an average speed of 131.456kph. Bracco was 28 minutes behind and Rol 44 minutes. This was Biondetti's fourth win in the Brescian race and it was to be his last. It was the second of the eight victories that Ferrari was to win in the Mille Miglia. The Commendatore had, however, realized that the Formula 1 car (the supercharged 125) was not a single-seater that could beat its opponents in the manner he wanted: decisively. Soon, in 1950, the Formula 1 drivers' world championship would start and Ferrari had to prepare something new and original. He knew above all that he had to give up the supercharged engine, as used by the 125 and the Alfa Romeo 158, which remained the car to beat: an exhilarating goal to be achieved.

Meanwhile, the exploits continued. The famous Le Mans 24 hour race was held in June. Luigi Chinetti raced in the Ferrari 2000 with the Englishman Lord Selsdon, but only gave him the wheel for a very short time, perhaps an hour. Chinetti won, with an average speed of 132.946kph, beating the Delages, the Aston Martins, the

45

Talbots, the Bentleys and the MGs.

This victory marked an important step for the factory. Ferrari proved that his cars were not just fast, but solid and durable too. Wealthy customers around the world began to notice Ferrari and he began to think that, in addition to racing-cars, he ought to produce GT road cars, to be sold to anyone who could afford such a luxury. There are wealthy people everywhere, but the cars from the Maranello factory could mostly go abroad, whilst those of Maserati, the other famous firm from Modena, were sold mostly in Italy.

The foreign market that has always absorbed the most Ferraris is that of the United States, but in recent years safety and anti-pollution laws have created difficulties for the Maranello factory. However, they are now ready to confront the severe and sometimes apparently absurd tests that are applied to cars imported into the USA. For several years, many Ferraris have gone to the Middle East, but customers have always been well distributed throughout the world. Owning a car made in Maranello has become one of the most obvious signs of success.

Maserati has always presented Ferrari with an effective competitor for world markets, but recent troubles have made it lose ground. I remember when a worker in a toll booth on the Autostrada del Sole told Ferrari that Maserati was the poor man's Ferrari. He promptly denied it but afterwards chuckled contentedly at me.

While Chinetti was winning in France, Manuel Fangio joined Ascari, Villoresi, Bonetto, Cortese and the others and started to race for Ferrari. He won the Monza Grand Prix, covering the 504km of the course (that was the distance of Grand Prix races at that time) at an average speed of 160.149kph in the 166 Formula 2.

The first five places all went to Ferrari cars.

Chinetti repeated his achievement at Le Mans by winning the Spa 24 hour race with Lucas at an average speed of 126.613kph.

Meanwhile, Mario Tadini, the unforgettable 'King of the Mountains' returned to Ferrari. He had bought dozens of the Scuderia Ferrari's Alfa Romeos, handing over huge sums to Ferrari and becoming one of his major supporters. Tadini entered the Circuito del Garda and came in second on the heels of Gigi Villoresi; in third place was an unknown young English driver, the 20-year-old Stirling Moss who was at the wheel of a tiny Cooper-Jap. When I saw that little spider coming round the bends near the lake, I couldn't believe my eyes and I certainly did not imagine that one day Moss would be one of the great drivers of the world and that the Cooper would become an excellent Formula 1 car, capable of winning world titles and giving Ferrari a sound beating.

The 1949 season ended with Ascari's victory – ahead of Fangio, Villoresi and Campos (all in Ferraris) – at the Grand Prix General Peron, a *formula libre* [free formula] race held in Buenos Aires on December 18th.

The year's results were 49 races, 30 wins, 18 second places, 12 third places. The successes were increasingly gratifying and Ferrari was becoming increasingly famous, but his goal was still a long way off.

6

The days of sweet revenge begin

T he year of 1950 was a significant one in the history of motor racing. As we have already said, it marked the start of the drivers' world championship for Formula 1 cars.

The formula was for single-seaters with 1500cc supercharged engines, or 4500cc normally-aspirated engines.

It was the beginning of a long and fascinating story of exploits of drivers and achievements of car makers. But it has also been a story of sorrow because of the accidents which killed so many courageous men; men who had chosen the motor car as their means of self-expression.

The racing season began in Argentina. The Ferrari team was impressive. Villoresi won two formula libre races and Ascari one, while the Mar del Plata sports car Grand Prix fell to the Argentinian Menditeguy, who was driving a Ferrari Mille Miglia. It was a good start.

Ferrari drivers were winning around the world, while at Maranello, work was being done on the future Grand Prix single-seater, the car that would have to beat the Alfa Romeo 158s. Ferrari and his men, including Aurelio Lampredi, the brilliant designer from Livorno who had joined Ferrari two years before, did not spare any effort. Innumerable hours were spent in the workshop. The Commendatore was in a hurry, but he knew that too much haste could bring trouble and he wanted no problems to hinder the arrival of the 'great day'.

Villoresi, Ascari, Fangio and Sommer, all in Ferraris, took the first four places in the Marseilles Grand Prix, held on the feast of San Giuseppe (March 19th). On the 10th April, Luigi Musso, who years later would become an official driver for Ferrari, won the Palermo-Monte Pellegrino hillclimb race in a 166 Mille Miglia. This was a day to remember. Tazio Nuvolari also took part in the race in an 1100cc Abarth 204 A spider.

Tazio was first in his class and fifth overall. It was to be his last win and his last race, though the legendary Nivola [Nuvolari] did not know it. He thought he would return to the world of Grand Prix racing with the Cisitalia 1500, designed by the ingenious Ferdinand Porsche. But it was not to be. The Cisitalia would never race, and Nuvolari would end his glorious career with a modest hillclimb race.

A few days before, Villoresi came second in the Sanremo Grand Prix, on the heels of Fangio's Alfa Romeo. The great duel which would decide things once and for all was drawing closer. Ferrari could feel it coming and could smell success in the forthcoming encounter.

On the 23rd April, the Mille Miglia started. There were 375 vehicles at the start and 213 of them would finish the course. In the front were Ferrari and Alfa Romeo. Ferrari had entered two 3300s driven by Ascari and Villoresi and two 2400s driven by Giannino Marzotto and Serafini, and ex-motorcycle champion like Varzi, Nuvolari and Alberto Ascari. Fangio, who was taking part in his first Mille Miglia, was at the wheel of an Alfa Romeo 2500, while Felice Bonetto was in a large 12-cylinder Alfa 4500 that was, however, not part of the official Alfa team.

The race had all the ingredients for a keenly-fought battle and there was to be no lack of drama and surprise. The course ran in clockwise direction, first the Adriatic coast, then the Tyrrhenian. At Ravenna, Giannino Marzotto went into the lead in his Ferrari berlinetta, with Crosara at his side. Giannino was wearing a blue suit and a tie. It made a strange impression to see this 'gentleman' amongst the other sportsmen in their various styles. Two other Ferraris were behind Marzotto, Villoresi-Cassani at a distance of two minutes and Serafini-Salani at three minutes. Bonetto was seven minutes behind, with Fangio sticking close to him. At Rome, Marzotto was still in front, with a 20 second lead over Serafini and a lead of more than 9 minutes over Fangio, who was always called the 'truck-driver' of road racing, because he always completed the course, whatever happened. Ascari, Villoresi and the others had dropped out of the race. At Livorno, the leading pair were ten minutes ahead of Serafini and a dozen ahead of Fangio. At the finishing line, the Marzotto-Crosara Ferrari was 7 minutes 33 seconds ahead of Serafini-Salani and 22 minutes 45 seconds ahead of the Alfa driven by Fangio, who was accompanied by Augusto Zanardi, the skilful test-driver from the Casa del Portello. Biondetti, at the wheel of a Jaguar, came in eighth, one hour behind the winners.

On the 7th May at the Modena '*Aerautodromo*' (far too grandiose a term for an installation that was never used for the purpose for which it was intended), the new Formula 2 Ferrari made its first appearance and took the first two places in the hands of Alberto Ascari and Mario Tadini. On the same day, Villoresi and Vallone and came in first and second in the Grand Prix of central Switzerland. Also on the 7th May, the first success in the United States was achieved. Briggs Cunningham won at Suffolk County airport. Ferrari was beginning to make a name for itself in the valuable American market.

Three wins in one single day – the Commendatore could be well satisfied.

On the 13th May, the British Grand Prix, the first contest in the Formula 1 world championship, was held at Silverstone. There was no Ferrari on the track, but the race was won by Nino Farina, who thus gained the driver's championship points.

The second world championship round was the Monaco Grand Prix on the 21st May. This time Ferrari was there with three single-seaters driven by Ascari, Villoresi and Sommer. Opposing them were three Alfa Romeos entrusted to the three Fs: Farina, Fagioli and Fangio. Unusually for him, Fangio shot into the lead right from the start. Towards the end of the first lap, the Argentinian went round the tobacconist's bend only to find his path blocked by a tangle of cars. Fangio almost came to a stop and, seeing a small gap on the right, went through it unscathed, gaining a lead which he kept until the end of the race. In second place was Alberto Ascari's Ferrari and fourth – behind the local favourite, Louis Chiron, in a Maserati – was Sommer in the other Ferrari. Later, Fangio told me that he owed his win to a photograph he had seen before the race. This had been on display at the tobacconist's and showed a scene from a race years before. The photograph showed a confused mass of cars in front of the famous shop.

Fangio said: 'When I saw the photo, I realized that the same thing could happen again. So I decided to shoot into the lead, so that nobody would be in front of me. And, indeed, almost at the end of the first lap, when I came out of the tunnel, I saw the yellow flag, warning me of the danger. I had been right. I went through and won. But without the photo, could I have done it? This is an example of the thoughtful approach that helped the Argentinian driver win five world titles.

Ascari's second place at Monaco was encouraging but, on the 4th June in the Swiss Grand Prix at Bern, Ferrari took a backward step when its three drivers had to withdraw.

In Belgium, two weeks later, the non-supercharged Ferrari with a capacity of a little more than 3200cc made its appearance. It was entrusted to Ascari, the leading driver in the team. The other Ferrari, the usual 12-cylinder 1500, was driven by Villoresi. The two came in fifth and sixth – although Villoresi had been faster in the trials, Ascari beat his companion in the race.

In France, the Ferraris that had taken part in the Grand Prix trials were not entered in the race.

On the 23rd July, Chinetti won the Paris 12 hour race again and the 20th August was the day of the German Grand Prix for Formula 2 single-seaters – a non-championship race. Alberto Ascari won it brilliantly and this was the first of the three successive wins he was to achieve on the difficult course. These three wins earned him the title 'maestro of the Nürburgring'.

The last round of the world championship was the Italian Grand Prix at Monza on the 3rd September. This time, Ascari was driving a 4500 – the car that was to give Ferrari great satisfaction, not immediately but in the following year . . . In practice, the first driver of the Modena team achieved the second best time, only a decimal point behind Fangio. Instead of Gigi Villoresi, who had had a bad accident in Geneva at the end of July, Ferrari entered Dorino Serafini Ascari went into the lead and showed the possibilities of the 4500, but then he was overtaken by Nino Farina, whose win gave him the world title.

Ascari came in second. Ferrari was now certain that the new single-seater had everything it needed to win and finally to beat the Alfa Romeos. A few weeks later, with the Alfas absent, Ascari, Serafini and Taruffi took the first three places in the Peña-Rhin Grand Prix at Barcelona. Another step forward had been taken.

The new Ferrari had thus produced its first successes. It had been carefully prepared by the tireless Luigi Bazzi. The 12 cylinder engine was arranged in a 60° V formation, with a bore of 80mm and a piston stroke of 74.5mm. The wet cylinder liners were screwed into the combustion chambers of the light alloy fixed-head engine block. Three 4 choke carburettors supplied the engine's fuel. There were two valves per cylinder and a dual ignition system. The single piece crankshaft, turned on seven thin shell bearings. There were two camshafts and a single-plate clutch. The new car also boasted a four-speed gearbox and De Dion rear axle. At 7500rpm, the engine generated 380 horsepower. The top speed was over 290kph. The 4500, which was designed by the imaginative Aurelio Lampredi, was descended from – the 2000cc engine which, fitted to a sports car, had won the Mille Miglia driven by Biondetti in the spring of 1948.

The 2000cc engine, which had been designed by engineer Gioacchino Colombo, had served as a basis for Lampredi's numerous experiments. At the beginning of 1950, the 3300cc 275/Mille Miglia and then the 4100 followed by the 4500 – all sports cars – were well-known. However, these cars were no more than the forerunners of a new Ferrari 4500 formula 1 car which was ready at the end of August, just before the Italian Grand Prix.

Ferrari had once more scored a bull's eye and his 4500 immediately showed itself to be capable of the required great achievement – beating the Alfa Romeo 158. Ferrari said: 'After years of unopposed domination by supercharged cars in Formula 1, the idea we have been developing – a normally-aspirated 12-cylinder engine of 4500cc-produced its first fruits. Progress was hard-going and the path to victory was spattered with blood – our dear Raymond Sommer has left us and we cannot conceal our grief.'

In 1950, the Ferrari company took part in 74 races, winning 46 of them. It achieved 33 second places and 18 thirds.

7

14th July 1951: a dream comes true

T he year of 1951 was an important one in the Ferrari story. In fact, I consider it to be the most important and decisive year.

It was in that year that the racing cars of the *Cavallino Rampante* [Prancing Horse] managed to overcome those of Alfa Romeo so that Ferrari could see his dreams fulfilled. Everything he would later attain – multiple wins, world titles, praise and prizes – would be the natural continuation of the successes achieved in 1951.

Beating the 158 was the task the man from Maranello had set himself in 1939 and when he finally achieved it, he would revel in the exhilarating victory.

The season began in February in Argentina, where two Grand Prix races were to be dedicated to Peron and his wife Evita. Both of them were formula libre and both of them were entered by the official Mercedes team, whose 3000s were being driven by drivers such as Fangio, Lang and Kling. The German single-seaters found that, apart from some Alfa Romeos and Maseratis, they were being opposed by two Ferraris that were an amalgam of proven design and novelty. A 166 engine – 2000cc, but supercharged – was mounted in a chassis that was destined for the future Formula 2 cars. The drivers were both Argentinians: Gonzales and Galvez. Gonzales won the first race ahead of Lang, Fangio and Galvez. He also took the second race in front of Kling and Lang, but Galvez had to retire.

The first confrontation between the new Ferrari cars and the well-tested Mercedes was therefore decided in favour of the cars from Modena and the applause of Italian racing enthusiasts gave

Ferrari a great deal of satisfaction. However, beating Mercedes was not his main purpose . . .

On the 11th March, the 432km track of the Siracusa Grand Prix was on Ferrari's schedule. Gigi Villoresi won the day in the 4500, which was getting faster and faster and which was the constant focus of Ferrari's attention.

The Giro di Sicilia, with its usual difficult 1080km course, was held on the 1st April. Two official 12-cylinder Ferraris, each with a capacity of 2562cc led the way to an overall win. They were driven by Vittorio Marzotto, Giannino's brother, and Piero Taruffi. Marzotto came first, just in front of the Roman driver and the third place was taken by Sergio Sighinolfi in a Stanguellini 1100. Years later, the excellent young driver would become a test-driver for Ferrari and would die during trials on the Modena Apennine road.

The 18th Mille Miglia was held on the 29th April. Two Ferrari America 340s (12 cylinder, 4101cc) were entrusted to Alberto Ascari and Gigi Villoresi. The three Marzotto brothers – Giannino, Vittorio and Paolo – also took part in the race, driving various other types of Ferrari. Early in the race Ascari went off the road after being dazzled by the headlights of a spectator's car and Giannino Marzotto quickly took the lead. Vittorio Marzotto dropped out at Fano and at Senigallia, it was Giannino who had to retire. Dorino Serafini, another Ferrari driver, had a bad accident at San Benedetto del Tronto and had to be taken to hospital.

The only Ferrari drivers left in the race were Gigi Villoresi and Paolo Marzotto, whose regular co-driver had for some time been Marino Marini, a war-time torpedo-bomber ace and a great friend of mine. The most dangerous adversary was Giovanni Bracco, who was driving the new Aurelia GT 2000, a car that was to become a fantastic road-racer. After Rome, Bracco started to gain on Villoresi. On the outskirts of Firenze, the Milanese driver had serious gearbox problems, which left him with only first and fourth gears. It was also pouring with rain. At Firenze, there were only 2 minutes 31 seconds between Villoresi and Bracco. But Villoresi managed to cross the Apennines with great skill, got up speed on the plain and won, with an average speed of 121.822kph. Scotti-Ruspaggiari's third place and Paolo Marzotto-Marini's fourth completed Ferrari's success.

However this Mille Miglia was most of all remembered because of the debut made there by the Lancia Aurelia GT with coachwork by Pininfarina. Bracco, who raced with Umberto Maglioli, was overall second, 'Ippocampo'-Mori fifth, Valenzano-Maggio seventh and Grolla-Monteferraio sixteenth. A magnificent result.

The first race in the drivers' Formula 1 world championship was the Swiss Grand Prix on the 27th May. The three Alfa 158s driven by Fangio, Farina and Sanesi were to be taken on by the Ferrari 4500s driven by Ascari, Villoresi and Taruffi.

Villoresi was on the front row of the grid. Fangio won, Taruffi came second and Ascari sixth. There was satisfaction in Maranello.

The second world championship event was the Belgian Grand Prix on the 17th June. The official teams entered by Alfa and by Ferrari were the same as in the Swiss race.

Villoresi was once more on the front row, next to Fangio, the fastest, in practice and to Farina. Farina won, with Ascari and Villoresi coming second and third respectively.

In the French Grand Prix, there was a fourth 158 for Fagioli and a fourth Ferrari for Gonzales. In practice, the fastest – after Fangio and Farina – was Ascari. In the race, Fangio and Ascari were disputing the lead but then both of them had to retire. However, the two of them got back into the race in single-seaters belonging to Fagioli and Gonzales respectively. Fangio came first, Ascari second and Villoresi third.

The 14th July was a glorious day for Ferrari. In France, they were celebrating the storming of the Bastille and at Silverstone, Ferrari was celebrating the greatest day in his life – both personal and professional . . .

Three Ferraris, driven by Ascari, Villoresi and Gonzales, had lined up against four Alfas, driven by Fangio, Farina, Sanesi and Bonetto. In practice, the fastest were Gonzales and Fangio, who had the same time, followed by Farina and Ascari. However, Gonzales was having one of his memorable days and Fangio did not manage to stand up to him. The duel between the two Argentinian drivers fascinated the spectators and a dependable Villoresi followed just behind them. At the finishing line, Gonzales beat Fangio by a good 51 seconds and Villoresi came third. The great, great day had come! Ferrari wrote: 'When in 1951, Gonzales unleashed himself on the 159 – the updated version of the 158 – and on the entire Alfa team leaving them behind. I wept with joy. But my tears of happiness were also mixed with tears of sorrow because, on that day, I thought "I have killed my mother".

Ferrari, Ferrari . . . how can we believe him? He had been waiting for this day for years: twelve to be precise. Tears of joy, yes, but not tears of sorrow for the defeated Alfa. I am more inclined to think that in those moments Ferrari was singing, with Othello: '*Credo in un Dio crudel che m'ha creato simile a sé* ['I believe in a cruel God who has created me in his likeness'].

The victory at Silverstone provided definitive proof that the Ferrari 4500 was an impressive car and that Gonzales, when he was in the right frame of mind, was a formidable opponent for anyone.

On the 20th and 22nd July, Giovanni Bracco won the Aosta-Gran San Bernardo and Susa-Moncensio hillclimbs in the Ferrari 4100.

The German Grand Prix was held at the Nürburgring on the 29th July. This was the day of the long-awaited 'return match' after the British Grand Prix. Racing enthusiasts were waiting with bated breath. The four Alfas driven by Fangio, Farina, Bonetto and Pietsch were confronted by five Ferraris, four dual-ignition 4500s driven by Ascari, Villoresi, Gonzales and Taruffi and a 212 driven by Fisher. The fastest in practice were Ascari and Gonzales, followed by Fangio and Farina. The race confirmed the Silverstone result and, in fact, enhanced it. Ascari won and Fangio came second in the only Alfa left in the race. Gonzales came third, Villoresi fourth, Taruffi fifth and Fisher sixth.

Ferrari's belief in the normally-aspirated engine – which also has the advantage of lower fuel consumption, consequently requiring fewer stops for refuelling – was therefore proved to be justified and Alfa had to admit as much.

From the 30th August to the 11th September, there was a Tour of France and three Ferrari 212 Exports took the first three places.

On the 2nd September at Bari, Taruffi introduced the new 2-litre 4-cylinder car, which would later become an illustrious single-seater. The Roman driver came in third behind Fangio's Alfa 159 and Gonzales' 4500.

Fifteen days later, Monza was the scene of the penultimate contest in the world championship. Excitement was at fever pitch and the public realized that this was to be an important day in the Alfa-Ferrari struggle. The Alfa 159s were driven by Fangio, Farina, Bonetto and De Graffenried, while Ascari, Villoresi, Gonzales and Taruffi were driving the Ferraris. Fangio and Farina were the fastest in practice, followed by Ascari and Gonzales. In the race itself, the Alfas at first seemed to have the upper hand, but the Modena team imposed its superiority. Ascari came first, Gonzales second, Farina (who had taken over Bonetto's car) third, Villoresi fourth and Taruffi fifth. The Maranello supporters went wild with delight and Ascari took himself to within three points of Fangio in the championship.

One week later, at Modena, Ascari and Villoresi tried out the new single-seater that had been prepared for the next Formula 2 season. This was the F.500/51, with a 2000cc, 4-cylinder engine. Gonzales was in another 2000. Ascari won, ahead of Gonzales.

The last round in the world championship was the Spanish Grand Prix on the 28th October. The Ferraris were driven by Ascari, Gonzales, Villoresi and Taruffi and the Alfas by Fangio, Farina, Bonetto and De Graffenried. The best time in practice was achieved by Ascari, followed by Fangio, Gonzales and Farina. The world title would be decided by this race, but the Ferrari team ran into troubles: mistakes had been made with tyre selection and the drivers were plagued by tyre problems.

Fangio won, Gonzales came second, Farina third, Ascari fourth, Bonetto fifth and De Graffenried sixth.

The world title thus went to Fangio and Ferrari had to make do with the second and third places awarded to Ascari and Gonzales. Years later, when I was talking to the great champion Nino Farina, I suggested that, for commercial reasons, Alfa had wanted Fangio to win the world championship and not him. The Turin driver would have none of it – according to him it had not been up to Alfa to decide, rather the result was determined by the abilities of the drivers.

Remembering 1951, Ferrari wrote: 'When, one month after Silverstone, Alberto Ascari, who was driving the same car [as at Silverstone], brought the same team [Alfa] to its knees at the Nürburgring, thereby revealing his incomparable class, I said sorrowfully: "It's over. Today Alfa Romeo has started to decline as a racing force, just like Fiat before it, which dwindled to the point of giving up."

'I was the one who brought Alfa the technicians it needed to snatch racing glory away from Fiat. When I left Alfa, I took no-one else with me, apart from my friend Bazzi, who had already been moved to one side by Ricart. As I left, I had the feeling that Alfa Romeo would lose its racing abilities because of me. And so it happened. I had witnessed or had taken part in, perhaps decisively, two momentous changes in the motor-racing world – one affecting Fiat and the other Alfa. I am not sorry about what happened, since I consider that my activities took the form of a modest service – at various times and in various amounts – to my country and to my colleagues, even if they arose from a selfish need to satisfy my competitive yearning.'

Though the 4500 may have given Ferrari the greatest feeling of satisfaction in his life, it also encouraged the creation of a British racing-car, the Vanwall. Ferrari himself provoked the building of this single-seater, which would later beat the Maranello cars, and decisively too.

Ferrari never sold single-seater racing-cars. He only ever sold sports cars to his customers. He always kept the single-seaters for himself, except once when he sold Tony Vandervell, the British thin-wall-bearing manufacturer, two or three cars, including a 12-cylinder 4500; in fact the very car that had achieved the feat of beating Alfa Romeo . . .

After arriving in Britain, the Italian 4500 became the 'Thin Wall Special' and took part in many races, though no world championship ones. One day, Vandervell arrived in Modena. As a Ferrari customer, since he had bought the 4500, and as a supplier of bearings to Ferrari, he wanted to meet the Commendatore. However, the latter was very busy and after three hours he had still not received the Englishman. Vandervell waited for another half hour, then left. That is what someone from the Ferrari company told me.

Tony Vandervell returned home and decided to make a racing car that could beat the Ferrari. It would be called Vanwall (a contraction of Vandervell and Thin Wall). In 1954, the first Vanwall appeared with a chassis inspired by the Ferrari, but the car did not produce results.

Vandervell wanted to win and money was no object to him. For his new chassis, he obtained the help of Colin Chapman, the maker of the light and stable Lotus sports cars. For the coachwork, he turned to Frank Costin – the man who would later found Cosworth motors, together with Keith Duckworth. The Vanwall's 4-cylinder engine was based on the Norton motorcycle engine and used Bosch fuel injection (Vandervell was following the example of Mercedes in this respect). The engine generated 290 horsepower at 7400rpm. The Vanwall's five-speed gearbox, which was rear mounted in unit with the differential, was similar to that of the Ferrari 4500.

When the Vanwall won, Ferrari showed me photographs of the British car and of his cars to prove to me that Vandervell had not hesitated to copy. As if it was uncommon for racing-car makers to look over each other's shoulders . . . !

The Vanwall took part in a couple of world championship contests in 1954 driven by Peter Collins, in five Grand Prix races in 1955 driven by Hawthorn, Schell and Wharton and then, in 1956, it was entrusted to Trintignant, Gonzales and Taruffi. But the results were disappointing.

Giovanni Lurani, who was a good racing-driver in the thirties, and later became a journalist, wrote in his *Storia delle macchine da corsa:* 'Meanwhile, the Vanwall was taking shape. This make had been created by C.A. Vandervell, a magnate of the British motor industry whose company was famous for its bearings. Vandervell had been a member of the BRM consortium and, sickened by the resulting fiasco, he had acquired some Ferrari cars to study their characteristics and finally created his own car. The 4-cylinder engine was derived from the famous Norton single-cylinder racing-motorcycle engine and it was designed by Lem Kosmicki. The block and the crankshaft were closely related to Rolls-Royce. The Vanwall was originally a 2000cc Formula 2 car with a square-stroke engine, (86 x 86 mm). Later the engine was bored to 91 x 86 mm, 2237cc, and finally to 96 x 86 mm, 2490cc and, with its Bosch direct fuel injection, it generated 270 horsepower at 7500rpm.

'In 1955 and 1956, this car alternated between excellent performances and disappointing failures, but it was later to dominate the Grand Prix races of 1957 and 1958.' Further on, Lurani wrote: 'Meanwhile, in Europe, two British makes entered the field with very modern cars – Vanwall and BRM. Tony Vandervell, whose Vanwalls had already revealed their capabilities, particularly as regards power, now wanted to perfect his cars and consulted Colin Chapman. The latter produced a new tubular lattice chassis, retaining the original front suspension (wishbones and helical springs) but radically modifying the rear suspension by using a large transverse leaf spring and a De Dion ´axle with an incorporated, five-speed and very light gearbox. The bodywork, which had a rather strange tall and rounded form, was the work of the well-known Frank Costin. During 1956, the Vanwalls suffered from a series of technical hitches – such as injection failure, problems with axle lubrication and jammed controls – as well as from the misfortune of running into multiple pile-ups, as at Monte Carlo and Reims, but would prove to be perhaps the fastest cars of the year and the best qualified to challenge the Italian monopoly.'

In 1957, Vandervell made use of Stirling Moss and Tony Brooks. The latter came second in Monaco. Then there were the retirements of Salvadori and Lewis-Evans in France. But on the 20th July at the Aintree circuit in England, Vandervell had his first real satisfaction. Moss and Brooks were on the front row of the grid and Lewis-Evans on the third. Moss took the lead, but was forced to retire. He then took over Brooks' car, re-entered the race in ninth position and went on to win.

In England, where Ferrari had inflicted its first defeat on Alfa Romeo, it in its turn was overcome by the Vanwall. England's green and pleasant land had suddenly become less pleasant for Ferrari. Moss also went on to win at Pescara and Monza.

In 1958, out of the ten Grand Prix races, the Vanwall won six and Ferrari and Cooper two each. Mike Hawthorn, Ferrari's standard-bearer, became world champion, beating Moss by one point. The latter added a win in the little Cooper to his three wins in the Vanwall (the other three were by Brooks). Hawthorn won only one Grand Prix, but it was his placings and fastest lap times (which then used to be rewarded with points) that won him the title.

Tony Vandervell therefore got his revenge on Ferrari, who called him the 'meteoric Vandervell' but also recognized that, without the British bearings, Ferraris would never have won a world championship.

The 4500 was also involved in one of Ferrari's 'adventures' – the Indianapolis 500 Mile Race. The Modena car maker only once took a direct part in it, in 1952. Alberto Ascari was at the wheel of the powerful 12-cylinder car. During the qualifying trials, the Milanese driver astonished everyone with his consistency and showed that he could compete with the American drivers as an equal. The Italian single-seater had only minor modifications for the famous oval and certainly could not aspire to win the race. It was a trial run, so that later a Ferrari, purpose built for this American race could later be brought to Indianapolis. Ascari held his ground well in the race but in the 40th lap, when he was in 7th position, his Ferrari lost a rear wheel and he had to retire.

Indy is still the only major race missing from Ferrari's list of wins.

8

Ascari wins the first world title

The Indianapolis 'failure' did not make too big a dent in 1952, which may be considered to be another historic year for the Modena company. Indeed, in that year, Ferrari won its first championship title, with the help of Alberto Ascari. The car was the Formula 1 2000. The world championshop was open to Formula 2 cars because of the withdrawal of Alfa Romeo, the extraordinary power of the Ferrari cars and the lack of real opponents.

The Ferrari 2000, designed by Aurelio Lampredi, had a 4-cylinder in-line engine with two overhead valves per cylinder and produced 180 horsepower at 7500rpm. The car had a 4-speed gearbox, a tubular chassis and a De Dion rear axle.

Albert Ascari thus became world champion in 1952 and would retain the title in 1953. In 1952, Ferrari won seven contests out of eight (it failed to win only at Indianapolis) and in 1953, it won seven out of nine, missing Indianapolis and losing the Italian Grand Prix, which was won by Fangio in a Maserati. Even for Ascari, this was an unrepeatable record – in two years, he had won 11 times out of 17, or 16, since he did not take part in the Indianapolis 500 in 1953.

The degree of success achieved by Ferrari in 1952 was huge: 109 entries, 95 wins, 47 second places and 33 third places. In addition to all the races won inside Italy and abroad, all the championships achieved in Italy and elsewhere, the Modena company was also successful in the Mille Miglia, which Giovanni Bracco won in the 250S. Bracco's achievement was surprising – he won the duel with Kling's Mercedes 3000, which had been lined up at the start with two other German cars driven by Caracciola and Lang. The encounter was memorable and on the Futa Pass Bracco gained a good six minutes on the German driver. A few months before he died, he told me how he had managed to beat Kling: 'At each bend, while my co-driver Rolfo held on tight, I saw in my mind's eye an SS platoon executing groups of partisans. Pure fury made me go faster and faster and that's how I won.' Poor Giovanni – he was a free man, an exceptional road-racer and a real Italian.

In 1962, ten years after the great event, Bracco went to Modena to commemorate the Mille Miglia victory. Ferrari gave him a watch as a present. Bracco later confided to a friend: 'A watch costing just a few thousand lire – and I gave him 600 million to race his cars. But no matter.'

The book I wrote commemorating Lancia's 70th anniversary included the following reference to Bracco: 'In 1951, Giovanni Bracco took part in the Mille Miglia in the 2000cc Lancia Aurelia B20 coupé, which had appeared just before the great Brescian race. When he tried out the car, Bracco immediately realized its excellent aptitude for road-racing. If it should later rain, wonders could be done.

'Quarter of an hour before the start, some "lucky" raindrops started to fall on Bracco's Aurelia, number 332. Partnered by young Umberto Maglioli (his apprentice, who would also one day become an excellent road-racer), Bracco covered the distance to Ravenna in 2 hours 20 minutes. The Aurelia was going wonderfully, helped by Bracco's courage and tenacity. They were in fourth position. At Rome, the Lancia people told them that they were in the first five or six overall.

Bracco's masterful driving along the tortuous 227km between Rome and Siena enabled him to beat Bornigia's Alfa Romeo 3500 by 2 minutes and Gigi Villoresi's big Ferrari by over 5 minutes, thereby halving his shortfall in the overall classification. At Firenze, there were only 2 minutes 31 seconds between the Ferrari and the Lancia. Vittorio Jano was waiting for them at Firenze. Bracco remembers: "Jano was careful not to tell us that we were second overall on the heels of Villoresi and Cassani in their 4-litre Ferrari. In fact, he kept us standing for as long as possible – he must have been very confident – he had me wash my face and carefully checked over the car. I told him to let me go, because I was impatient to be off."

'Judging by the enthusiasm with which the crowd welcomed the

B20 on the approach to Brescia, Bracco thought he was first in his class. His words again: "On the final straight in via Rebuffone, I satisfied a whim: The usual 'experts' used to say that the Aurelia had no brakes. I crossed the finishing line, gave the brake pedal three short pumps and came to a stop. If anyone needed convincing, they were convinced now. Franco Bocca rushed up and embraced me. His spectacles were all steamed-up. He shouted that we were second overall. I had a dry throat since I had not had a drop to drink for more than 13 hours. I told him to fetch me a bottle of red wine so that we could drink a toast. But I drank it all myself." A few minutes later, Maglioli made a calculation: between Brescia and Brescia he had lit 140 cigarettes for Giovanni Bracco, his maestro.'

In 1952, Enzo Ferrari, who was then 54 years old, was nominated a *Cavaliere del Lavoro* [an Italian decoration awarded to important figures in industry]. He had been a very young *Cavaliere* [Knight] and a very young *Commendatore* before the war and now he was being 'promoted' yet again.

On the occasion of the nomination, the publication *Artefici del Lavoro Italiano* said: 'Ferrari is synonymous with industry – if that word may be used to describe the most perfect and the most personal achievements of a craftsman. In 1918, at the end of the First World War, Ferrari joined a workshop in Turin, so that he could live at the heart of the great adventure of motorization, which had been given a great push by the war. He remained in Turin for barely one year. Milan offered better possibilities and in the capital of Lombardy the young and enthusiastic engineer was able to fulfil his greatest dream – to race in a fast car. Early success enabled him to join Alfa as a racing-driver and he stayed with them for 20 years. This was a fundamental stage of his life, in which his instinctive knowledge of engines took shape, developed and was perfected. He became a man of iron will who knew no limits to his lofty aspirations.

'He gradually took over management of the racing department. When Alfa Romeo decided to close it down, Enzo Ferrari could not resign himself to abandoning the world for which he had lived, hoped and suffered. He started making his own cars and they won races. The adolescent dream, which had matured during his youth and had then been consolidated by years of racing and technical experience, had become a reality.'

64

Ferrari himself was no doubt the first to snort at so triumphalist a tribute. But then, you don't look a gift horse in the mouth.

1953 was also a magical year for the drivers and cars of the Cavallino Rampante. Success followed success on all tracks and circuits, in both speed and endurance races. As well as Ascari's world title, Ferrari also took the world racing-car constructors' title, which he had already won in 1952. Describing the two great years of 1952-53, the British journalist Gordon Wilkins wrote: 'Ferrari's supremacy was undoubtedly due to his courage, his foresight, his technical intuition and his organizational talents. But he always had a first-rate team of technicians, designers and mechanics and a remarkably well-equipped factory at his disposal. The best proof of the capabilities of the Formula 2 Ferrari was provided by Farina's win at the Nürburgring, with an average speed of 135kph. This average was faster than that of Ascari, who won in 1951 in the Formula 1 4500, and better than Caracciola, who won in 1937 in the big 5-litre Mercedes with an average speed of 133.2kph.

'All in all, the Formula 2 cars represented a considerable step forward in racing-car technology; apart from anything else, this was the first time in the history of the automobile that multi-cylinder engines had generated 100 horsepower per litre – a degree of power that had only ever been achieved by single-cylinder motor-cycles.'

Ferrari was still savouring the joy and satisfaction of his achievements when he received some worrying news – Ascari and Villoresi were leaving him and taking Eugenio Castellotti with them. The latter was not yet an official Ferrari driver, but he was a customer who had bought car upon car. This was a severe blow for Ferrari, but he had learnt how to hold his ground and to counter-attack. Indeed, it could be said that their departure – they joined Lancia – gave him increased strength and a stronger will to recover.

But why did Ascari leave? People have offered many suggestions. Some maintain that it was Gianni Lancia's money that persuaded him and Villoresi to join the Turin squad. Others consider that the two drivers were attracted not so much by money as by the fact that the Formula 1 Lancia had been created by Vittorio Jano, for whom Ascari and Villoresi had the highest regard. In view of the new formula which came into force in January 1954 (2500cc normally-aspirated engines or 750cc supercharged engines), Ferrari did not seem to have the car to repeat the exploits of the previous years. But this still does not explain why the faithful Ascari should hurriedly leave Ferrari at the first opportunity. What happened to his affection and respect? Is it possible that Ferrari did not know how to treat him? I never mentioned this 'betrayal' to Ferrari, but I know that he would have told me that he could not have competed with Lancia's money.

On the other hand, Villoresi maintains that money had nothing to do with it. The departure was caused by the behaviour of the Ferrari company. 'They wouldn't tell us what we would be doing in 1954. They produced no programmes and said not a word, causing us to waste a lot of time. So Ascari and I went to Modena. Ferrari received Alberto and I stayed to talk to Ugolini, but we got nothing out of them. We left Modena and stopped on the way home to call Gianni Lancia and tell him we were ready to sign up with him. Then we told Ferrari.'

Villoresi is too much of a gentleman not to be telling the truth and his account of his only appearance in the Indianapolis 500 in 1946 also has to be believed. In the post-war period, the Milanese champion was the only European member of the '100 mile an hour club', which consisted of drivers who had finished the race with an average speed of over 100mph, or 160kph. In the 1946 race, Villoresi drove his Maserati masterfully but was forced to stop several times because of magneto problems. He lost almost 40 minutes and was placed seventh, 36 minutes behind Robson, the winner. It is therefore obvious that he could have won. Gigi has always told me that his most fearsome adversary on that day was in fact boredom. Lap upon lap at the same speed, no gear changes, more than four hours on an oval track little more than four kilometres long. 'I found it hard to struggle against the indescribable boredom and tiredness caused by the relentless rhythm and the unchanging noise of the engine.' This is how this driver, who was excellent both on the racing track and on the road, remembers one of the great days of his career.

The sale of Ferrari cars to wealthy customers around the world had now got into its stride. In 1947, 7 Ferraris were sold, the next year 45 and between 1950 and 1955, production rose to 70-80 GT cars per year, all of which were of course snatched up by aspiring owners. People all over the world waited for months to get their

Ferrari. Famous people, princes, actors, rich heirs and heiresses all converged on Modena, in the hope of seeing their Ferrari being built and of spending some time with the Commendatore. But Ferrari, who once described Maranello as a 'disaster', kept himself out of the way. He knew who to receive and how to receive them. The public relations expert and enchanting talker made himself available only when it was worth his while and he was particularly prone to keeping away from racing-driver customers. Perhaps they wanted to race for Ferrari, in which case it was better not to hear their dreams and expectations.

One day when I was at lunch with Ferrari and Castellotti, Eugenio expressed his surprise that I was able to see the Commendatore whenever I wanted. He added: 'Even after I had bought seven Ferraris I couldn't see him. I had to become one of his drivers to be able to shake his hand.'

In 1954, Ferrari offered his customers the 250 Europa, a car that would become a reference point for his refined products, and he entered the 750 Monza and the 500 Mondial in races. Having lost Ascari and Villoresi, he relied on such drivers as Farina, Gonzales, Hawthorn and Maglioli for Formula 1 and the sports car races. To this list were added the customer-drivers, among whom the foremost were of course the Marzotto brothers. Fangio, the great adversary, started the Grand Prix season with Maserati and immediately won the first world championship contest at home in Argentina.

Ascari and Villoresi were champing at the bit. The great Alberto came first in the Mille Miglia. He had never liked this race – nor any other road race – but this time he had to enter it. Lancia, for whom Fangio had won the *Carrera Messicana* [Mexican Road Race] the year before, were now after success in the Mille Miglia too. Despite his dislike for this event, Ascari managed to win. Vittorio Marzotto was second in a Ferrari and Clemente Biondetti was fourth in another Ferrari. The Maranello company was recovering and won the Le Mans 24 hour race with the Gonzales-Trintignant partnership, who drove their 4900 to victory with an average speed of 169.215kph, beating the great Jaguar. Also in 1954, Umberto Maglioli won the Mexican Carrera for Ferrari, covering the 3077km of the course at an average speed of 173.702kph. Phil Hill, who would later become world champion with Ferrari, came second, Franco Cornacchia came fifth and Luigi Chinetti sixth. These last two were incomparable sellers of Ferraris, Chinetti in France and then the United States and Cornacchia in Italy. Franco was a good driver, but I think he gave the best of himself to his efforts to sell Ferraris. He made me laugh when he told me how difficult it was to win customers in the early days of the Maranello company. He said: 'In fact, in order to convince my customers, I had to pick up my gun, otherwise they wouldn't listen to me.'

On the 4th July a strong Mercedes team appeared at the French Grand Prix. Fangio, Kling and Hermann were all included. It was an awful day for Ferrari. His cars were no longer as competitive and, although he had excellent drivers, he would have needed a particularly outstanding young driver in order to make an impact. However, of course, Ferrari did not give in. He knew that the Germans were very powerful and that the other competing makes were also serious challengers. He continued on his course, with his head down, shouting away from dawn to dusk. He even shouted when talking would have been enough. But shouting does not get you very far. Mercedes started to carry off win after win, leaving Ferrari and the other car-makers very little. Nevertheless, the cars from Maranello managed to win two races, despite the Mercedes – Gonzales took the British Grand Prix and Hawthorn took the Spanish one, which was the last of the season. Ascari even raced a Ferrari at one event, at Monza in the Italian Grand Prix. In practice, he was amongst the fastest – Fangio's Mercedes and the Maserati driven by Stirling Moss. However, in the race itself, Ascari was forced to retire.

Later in Barcelona, he went to the front in his Lancia, and managed to build up a good lead, but he had to retire again.

Fangio, who had won the first two Grand Prix races of the year (Argentina and Belgium) for Maserati, continued his success with Mercedes and became world champion. Few will remember that his title was also due to the firm from Modena [Maserati].

Although the drivers' world title went to Fangio, the constructor's title went once again to Ferrari – which had won the Carrera Messicana with Maglioli, who was competing in his last race. The record of the Cavallino Rampante continued to be satisfactory.

In 1955, both the drivers' and the constructors' world titles went to Mercedes. Fangio was world champion for the third time and the German company also won in the sports car category. However, Moss beat Fangio in the Mille Miglia, achieving a record average speed. After the race, I interviewed the Argentinian champion, who told me quite candidly that before Pescara one of the injectors in the 8-cylinder engine had failed, so that he had to go from Pescara to Rome and then back to Brescia with his engine running on just seven cylinders. This is why he was called the 'truck-driver' – he always finished the race.

Of the six world championship Formula 1 contests, Ferrari only won the Monaco Grand Prix. The Mercedes were forced to retire, as was the Lancia in which Ascari was leading, leaving the field open for Trintignant to win for Ferrari. At the beginning of the stretch alongside the harbour. Ascari went into the water. He escaped without serious injury and a few days later he went to Monza where Ferrari were conducting trials for the coming Supercortemaggiore Grand Prix. He felt the need to return to the wheel and asked Castellotti to give him the Ferrari for a few laps. He set off and he never came back. On the bend before the stretch in front of the stands, the Ferrari overturned trapping Ascari beneath it. The car then rolled back on to its wheels and ended up on the left hand side of the track.

When I arrived on the scene, there was a long blue line on the asphalt. It had been made by Ascari's blue shirt which had dragged along the ground whilst he was trapped inside the cockpit with the car upside-down. Why did Ascari die? The answer is unclear.

Some say that the great champion was trying to avoid a workman who was crossing the track. He braked hard so as not to run the workman down and then lost control. Ferrari repeated this version in his memoirs, but he certainly could not swear to it. Ascari's death meant that Italian motor-racing lost its standard-bearer, that Lancia gave up racing, that Villoreso retired and that Castellotti joined Ferrari once and for all.

Cruel fate had meant that Ascari died at the wheel of one of the Ferrari's whose team he had left to drive for Lancia. A few days later Bill Vukovich, the Indianapolis ace, died in the Indy 500 during an attempt at his third consecutive win – an achievement that no driver had yet managed. 1955 was the most tragic year of all in the motor-racing world. In May Ascari and Vukovich died and in

June there was the tragedy at Le Mans, where 80 people died and 200 were injured.

My career as a journalist meant that I was also present during that sad episode at Le Mans and it is not easy to forget what I saw on the evening of 11th June 1955. It was the worst birthday of my life.

9

All eyes fixed on the road to Turin

W hile Mercedes was winning race after race, something important happened in Turin. Lancia gave up racing. It was then that an initiative took place that allowed Ferrari to continue racing with fewer worries, at least as far as finance was concerned.

Lancia handed over all its racing equipment to Ferrari and Fiat guaranteed Ferrari the sum of 250 million lire to be paid over five years at 50 million per year.

In July 1955, when the television news showed pictures of the handing over of Lancia equipment to Ferrari in the courtyard of the Torinese factory, the commentator's voice was cracked with emotion. I was the person reading the commentary, which I had also written. It was a sad afternoon. Enzo Ferrari was of course not present, he was at Modena. If he had been at Turin, he would have had to give his thanks and that would be done better by his envoys. A few days later he was at Grazzano Visconti for the funeral of Prince Caracciolo's wife, the mother-in-law of Giovanni Agnelli. When he had to present his condolences, he also gave thanks for the most welcome 250 million lire donation. As always, this was a hasty thank you, given almost grudgingly. It would be too much of an effort to say it loud and clear. The Lancia material was priceless; though some have put its value at near a thousand million lire.

Apart from this and apart from the fresh money from Fiat, Ferrari had another piece of good news. Mercedes, having won both the world drivers' title and the world constructors' title, withdrew from these forms of motorsport. Ferrari could now continue along his path with greater peace of mind.

Mercedes gave as their reason for retiring the fact that they had achieved all that they had set out to do. In two years, they had won everything that could be won and had created the legend of their formidable capabilities and organisational skills.

Mercedes had become synonymous with 'the car that wins' and so it was better to withdraw from competition, in case one of its adversaries should grow strong and create problems. Can we blame the German company? Today Mercedes is still living on the legend created in the years 1954-55, even though it does not mention it directly in its publicity. The secret is not just to win, but to know when to stop.

In this respect it is worth returning to the 1955 Le Mans, the most tragic race of all time, where 80 people were killed and 200 injured.

I can still recall vividly what I saw on that fateful evening. Levegh's Mercedes flying through the crowd, the dead, the ambulances on the track, the cars continuing to race in obedience to that sporting imperative that says 'the race must go on'. Then at nightfall, strips of black cloth appeared on the Mercedes pit in homage to the dead. In the dark, Fangio's Mercedes was leading but towards two o'clock in the morning the German company announced it was withdrawing as a sign of mourning.

Jaguar's win was thus overshadowed by the withdrawal of the silver German cars. It has been said in some quarters that the two Mercedes driven by Fangio-Moss and Kling-Simon withdrew because they were on their last legs. Who can tell whether or not this is true?

Before moving on from 1955, let us read what Ferrari wrote about some aspects of the year.

'The result of a race is fifty per cent due to the car. When the car has been made, you are only half way there. You now have to find a driver and it costs more to train a good racing-driver than it does to make a car. When I decide to take part in a race, I don't think about my competitors. I try to do my best, without telling myself "I must beat Mercedes or Maserati". For me, the importance of a race is the technical result, that is, whether – given the same course and the same atmospheric conditions – established records have been broken. If so, progress has been made.'

It sounds like an attempt to reduce the importance of defeats . . .

Ferrari also wrote: 'I am continually afflicted by inner suffering and when I entrust a car to a driver and shake his hand in the courtyard, I always think that perhaps I will be attending his funeral in a few days time. When Ascari died, I did not sleep for a long time. He was like a son. If I had not built racing cars, would so many of my friends be dead? If drivers worked out the risks, they would never race. Enthusiasm and passion, not profit or ambition, are the driving force behind racing-drivers and the manufacturers of racing cars.'

But drivers die and manufacturers do not.

After Le Mans, Ferrari wrote, but did not publish, the following: 'What were the causes of the accident? The secret and obstinate desire of many organizers to make their courses ever faster, so that they can say that their circuit is the fastest in Europe or the world. Encouraging the public to want greater thrills. Grandstands and pits in the most dangerous places. In 1936-37, under the rules of the weight limit, formula cars with engines of 5-6 litres, capable of speeds of over 300kph, could compete in races with a high average speed on circuits with straight stretches of 7-8 kilometres which, to avoid the consequence of possible tyre trouble, were interrupted by solid chicanes made, not of bales of straw, but of sand bags reinforced with wood. It is necessary to grade circuits, to create races for cars of similar engine capacities and to be convinced that the public will be greatly interested not only if the average speeds are astounding but, above all, if there is technical and sporting equivalence between the competitors.

But why not refuse to race on the more dangerous courses? Because, in practice, this would mean not racing at all and Ferrari was not a man to give up competition: he knew very well that standing still would mean losing precious time compared with his competitors and it would also mean giving up substantial engagements. Refusing the danger presented by some courses would therefore require certain technical and material sacrifices and this was something Ferrari could not accept. We may well criticize him, but we must accept his way of thinking, however reluctantly.

On the 19th September, 1955, Ferrari noted: 'Formula 1, which comes to an end on the 31st December 1959, has not exhausted its technical possibilities, although in the first two years great technical and sporting results have already been achieved. In fact, the times of the 1500 supercharged engine and the 4500 normally-aspirated engines have in most cases been surpassed. It is undisputable that races reserved to Formula 1 cars should continue, since they are the vanguard of an experimental area of improved mechanical creations and an irreplaceable test bench. Their suppression would only slow down or tame the rate of progress.

Strike while the iron is hot – racing also means making money. The year 1956 was kind to Ferrari. Mercedes and Lancia had disappeared and only Maserati, spearheaded by the great Stirling Moss, stood up to the red single-seaters from Maranello.

Ferrari entered the Lancia D50, which he had inherited from the Turin company in the July of the previous year, in the drivers' world championship. Though these cars were designed by Vittorio Jano, his dear friend whom he held in high regard, Ferrari could only say: 'There is something good in these cars' Nice of him! It would be too much for him to acknowledge how original and effective the Lancia single-seaters were.

There were six contests in the world championship and the Lancias, which were gradually modified and updated, won four races for him – three with Fangio and one with Collins.

The other two Grand Prix races went to Moss in his Maserati.

Ferrari had a large squad of drivers at his disposal and, during the year, could rely on Fangio, Castellotti, Musso, Collins, De Portago and Gendebien.

At the age of 45, Fangio won the world title for the fourth time, but he and Ferrari really did not get on with one another.

Ferrari, while recognizing the great qualities of the Argentinian driver, accused him of always managing to choose the best car and Fangio described the car-maker as a 'Richelieu'. He thus recognized Ferrari's great ability to turn any situation to his advantage and to get out of awkward corners.

Ferrari was a master in the art of dealing with men. Years later in December 1976, the ex-world champion went to Maranello to talk to Ferrari about the 1977 Argentinian Grand Prix. Before meeting the Grand Old Man, he confided to someone that he was ready to argue with Ferrari. However, after the visit, he said: 'What argument? He is still the same: youthful, cunning, agreeable. He decides what he wants and I accept what he will do.' No doubt the great Fangio had also mellowed with the years.

But the Argentinian was not the only one who had compared Ferrari to characters from history. Also in December 1976, Bernie

Ecclestone, the Brabham boss, who was called the 'Godfather' of Formula 1 because he represented the car manufacturers, said: 'He's the most incredible man I have ever met and I have known a lot of people. He's a legend, he's like Winston Churchill. People will always talk about him and I hope he lives to 200 years.'

Personally, I am not very convinced by this wish. Without Ferrari around, Ecclestone could be even more uninhibited than he is said to be.

10

Dino's death puts out the flame

At the end of January 1956 I was at Modena. It was then that Ferrari asked me if I, and my television colleagues, had come 'by means of the six-legged dog', i.e. AGIP. Years later, when Shell left the Italian market, Ferrari would race under the patronage of AGIP, but by that time the past would have been set aside. All that mattered was to be able to race.

When I started to meet Ferrari more often, I began to delight in the friendship that he offered me.

I studied him and I listened to him and he realised the value of having a friend who was a faithful journalist in a delicate and powerful sector of the media such as television.

Ferrari was the complete boss, a man with an excellent memory and a brilliant conversationalist, in fact he was the male equivalent of a siren. His silver hair and imposing figure commanded respect and few people could really get to know him. He dressed with dignity, but it was plain that no woman saw to his clothes.

It is surprising to see him in a photograph from 1955 at the wheel of one of his sports cars in a blue jacket and yellow pullover – the colours of Modena. He was a man who paid no attention to fashion, even though he knew people who sold the most refined items in Bologna. On his wrist, he was wearing a chronometer, which was already quite old and which had a black Cavallino Rampante on the face. I would have given a lot for that watch and Ferrari knew it. In his usual way, he never gave it to me and continued to wear that same watch for years. He was wearing a brick-red overcoat and a dove-grey hat, which he would keep for years. In his buttonhole the badge of the Scuderia caught the eye. This was a gold triangle with the Prancing Horse in the middle and the Italian flag on top.

The first months of 1956 were a long period of distress for Ferrari. Dino, his only son, who was 24 years old, was ill and nearing death. Ferrari was in a state of constant torment. Dino died in the Modena family home on the 30th June. On the next day, the Ferrari drivers raced in the French Grand Prix wearing black armbands. Collins won.

If he had, after Dino, ten other sons Ferrari would not have been as close to any of them as he was to Dino. Not because Dino was the first-born, but because the poor boy's suffering brought them closer together, as if he, the father, were responsible for the long, exhausting agony. When he talked about it – which he rarely did, apart from alluding to some episode or memory – it was obvious that the death was with him at all times. Some have said that Ferrari sometimes dwelt too much on Dino's illness and death and some have even claimed not to believe in all his grief, because he flaunted it too much. There is sometimes a thin line between what is permissible and what is excessive and it is certainly not up to me to make a judgement, especially since I also know the anxieties of fatherhood.

On the 16th July, he wrote to me in his violet ink: 'Dear Rancati, Thank you for your affectionate and understanding letter. I can no longer attach importance to remarks and criticisms. After the suffering I have been through, I now find irrelevant everything that would have greatly annoyed me and made me retaliate in the past. I will go on to the end of this season, and then I have decided to leave others the honour of better defending the interests of Italian industry abroad. It is important in life to know how to give up something that really matters to us and I think that, now I have lost my son, I could not and do not have anything more dear to me to give up. I hope to see you soon. Kindest regards. Ferrari.' Ferrari the rock had been shattered, but he found in his work a reason to go on. Even if he threatened to stop, anyone who knew him well knew that he would never to able to stop racing. That would mean the end of everything.

His black tie was the outer sign of his mourning. He would wear it for years, until he eventually reverted to pale-coloured ties, at which point, for some unknown reason, he also stopped wearing the Cavallino badge. One day when we were in Modena together, I very cautiously suggested to him that he might need a new pair of shoes.

He looked at the ones he had on and his mouth twisted. He reappeared about an hour later and proudly showed me a pair of new brown shoes. I told him that black ones would have looked good too. His mouth twisted again. He came back with a box under his arm – he had also brought some black ones. Then he saw my spectacles. He wanted to know where I had bought them: so the optician in Via Montenapoleone, Milan gained another customer.

Ferrari preferred dark lenses and used them even in winter. It was a way of observing without giving himself away.

After many years, he gave up his style of wearing trousers which were slightly too short and with underwear showing above the belt. He suddenly dressed decidedly better, as if a woman were taking care of him. His clothes were of pale colours and he did not wear an overcoat in the winter, just waterproof lined jackets. He never wore rings or tie-pins. He even started to look younger in the way he dressed. His ties gradually became more daring. One day he told me that he received too many of them as presents. He smiled and whispered to me: 'It's possible they don't realize that I would prefer whisky, good whisky.' Enzo Ferrari was also a gourmet and a connoisseur. There were often delicious surprises at his table. He never made a mistake and was very choosey and demanding. He was particularly well informed about wine and on his table he would keep a list of the ones he could offer his guests. He would accept what his guests chose, without trying to influence them and liked to be praised for his cellar.

In 1964, when the Ferrari cars entered the United States Grand Prix painted white and blue (the colours of Luigi Chinetti's North American Racing Team) because the 'man from Maranello' had 'declared war on Italy', the Cavallino was toasted with Formula Uno, a cocktail invented by Ferrari. This agreeable drink was a red colour. As Ferrari said, 'My cocktail at least should be red, since the cars have had to change colour.' Formula Uno is still drunk today and it is still just as good and invigorating.

In October 1956, Ferrari wrote to me '(by typewriter): 'Dear Rancati, I have received your letter of the 28th September and I am sorry to learn that you are unwell. I hope that you will soon be able to return to your work. I shall have to come to Cremona shortly and I shall ask after you. I have still not made up my mind about the future, but in a few days time I will be obliged to take decisions about the general situation as regards drivers, tyres, accessories and everything else that has to do with the world of motor-racing. Best wishes.'

So Ferrari had changed his mind somewhat. Time had influenced his decision about whether to withdraw from racing. He was already thinking of the future and that was the best sign that it would be possible to rely on him once more. My illness had been the grounds for a 'punishment' that was unjustly inflicted on me and Ferrari, along with my mother and father, was the only person to help me – he gave me work. At the end of the year, he wanted me with him during the organization of the annual press conference. I spent day after day at Modena, I gave a hand and I learnt many things. When Ferrari offered me payment, he did it very discreetly and tactfully.

For the next five years, from 1957 to 1961, he gave me the job of writing articles for the *Rivista Ferrari* [the Ferrari magazine] and of looking through other publications.

In 1956, Fangio was world champion. He once said to Roberto Bonetto, the esteemed journalist and son of the great Felice, 'What a car the Formula 1 Lancia is. It's ten years ahead of the Mercedes.' The Argentinian had already decided to leave Ferrari and he joined Maserati. The reasons for this are unclear. Perhaps his relations with Ferrari and with the other members of the team led to the split or perhaps Maserati's terms were much better than Ferrari's?

In his memoirs, Ferrari writes: 'In 1956, Manuel Fangio raced in the official Ferrari team. He had already been world champion three times. He took part in fifteen races, winning six of them, coming second in four, fourth in two and retiring from three. That season he became world champion for the fourth time. But, according to his memoirs, 1956 had consisted of a series of betrayals, plots, tricks and breathtaking machinations all intended to undermine him. And who was responsible for the treacherous manoeuvres? – Enzo Ferrari, the very man who had taken him on.' Ferrari goes on to demolish one by one the accusations made by the Argentinian champion. He continues: 'But why should Enzo Ferrari, the Metternich – or even the Richelieu – of the automobile world, try with such treacherous cunning to ruin the best man in his team, the world champion? Fangio has no doubts about this and he explains it as follows: "Ferrari wanted above all to show that his cars could win even without the world champion at the wheel. Secondly, he wanted Peter Collins to win the world title, because

Collins would mean sales in Britain, while the Argentinian market at that time was closed to imports." '

After some further comments, Ferrari concludes: 'It thus takes all one's courage to define oneself as being "rejected by Ferrari" as Manual Fangio says he is, forgetting the sacrifice of his team-mates. What should I conclude from this? Fangio was a great driver who was afflicted by a persecution complex. In fact, it was not just against me that he harboured suspicions: he himself says that in one race Villoresi skidded on purpose so as to collide with his car, with the aim of helping his friend Ascari; another time, he accused the Alfa mechanics of deliberately not filling up his fuel tank so that Farina would win. On other occasions he explained his failures – at the Nürburgring and Silverstone – by saying that he had not been given a suitable Alfa Romeo. Manuel Fangio's persecution complex sometimes becomes quite farcical. He says that on the night before the 1957 Monaco Grand Prix, he received in his hotel a perfumed note containing the room key of a "beautiful Parisian film actress who is now a star". He did not take the bait, had a good night's sleep and the next day he won. All credit to the well-known incorruptibility of the champion. But that is not all. The champion then suspects that the beautiful temptress was sent to him by competitors as a trap. Now, in that year Fangio was racing for Maserati and the only real rival was Ferrari. It is easy to see who would have been held responsible for such an infernal plot.

'A strange character. I have had to reply here to all his insinuations, but I have done it without rancour, with a smile on my lips. In any case, none of this changes my opinion of the man at the wheel of a racing car. In fact I think it will be difficult for me to find another ace capable of such continual success. Fangio has never embraced any cause. Conscious of his abilities, he has always pursued every chance of driving the best car of the day. He has been successful in this, by putting his – legitimate and natural – egoism before the affection that bound other great drivers to one make, in good times and bad. But he has always struggled, not only for first place, but also to be included at the other end of the place-list, so that he could at least have taken the car as far as the finishing line. This is the noble trait that I recognize in him.'

Ferrari wrote this in 1962. Of the time he knew Fangio, he remembers: 'At a certain point, I started to look at him with puzzlement. Was he shy, mediocre, cunning? I did not understand him. He didn't look me in the eye, answered in monosyllables with a strange tinny kind of voice and was quick to let others speak on his behalf, while a constant, indefinable smile would make his face become impenetrable.'

In view of the above, it is not difficult to imagine the reasons for the split: two strong personalities trying to show who most deserved success.

On the 2nd December 1956, the first contact between the drivers and the Formula 1 cars took place on the track at Modena. They were young drivers – Castellotti, Collins, De Portago, Hawthorn, Musso, Perdisa, Von Trips – and, in the course of the year, Evans, Gendebien, Phil Hill, Severi and Trintignant were added to their number.

I dubbed the line-up as the 'Ferrari Spring'. They were magnificent young fighters. They wanted to race and they wanted to win.

Eugenio Castellotti took me by the arm and asked me to go with him to inspect a change in the bend before the pits. He seemed troubled and I told him so. He replied: 'You're right. I'm at a tricky stage in my life. Delia [his fiancee] wants me to stop racing and I want her to give up the stage. I'm ready to give up, but she wants me to be the only one to say goodbye to the great passion in my life.' What could I say to him? I reminded him that what his profession required above all was serenity. I noticed a far-away look in his eyes. I would never see him again. In March, Eugenio was killed during a test run at Modena. A few days later Ferrari would have gone to Lodi to see *Signora* Angela, the driver's mother, in an attempt to persuade her to change the position she had adopted regarding her son.

In the middle of January 1957, Ferrari wrote to me: 'I have received your letter on the 14th . . . Up till now, no other friend, apart from the *Gruppo Sportivo di Rezzato,* has remembered Ferrari. However, the races have only just started and I still put my trust in my workshop and in my drivers.'

He was just the same. He had not given up. He had rolled up his sleeves and set to work, with absolute faith in his men, young and old, in the workshop and on the track.

11

The Mille Miglia and the great fear

A nother year of mourning was 1957. In March Ferrari lost Castellotti and in May there was an accident during the last few kilometres of the Mille Miglia. The race headquarters of the team was at Manerbio, between Cremona and Brescia, and it was there I stayed on the night before what was to be the last Mille Miglia. I remember seeing the head mechanic Marchetti being subject to Piero Taruffi's fussiness. The Roman driver, who was 51 years old and was making his 15th appearance in the long distace race, felt that it might be the last time he would be able to try to win this contest that had obsessed him. He left no stone unturned in preparing both himself and his car for victory.

On the 12th May, I was 'on duty' with my friend Carlo Facchetti at Piacenza. Where the course of the race leaves the Via Emilia and turns towards Cremona, there is a bend, at the entrance to which is a Shell station. Facchetti and I were charged with giving the official Ferrari drivers their positions and any messages. We received communications by telephone at the service station.

In the afternoon, the telephone rang. It was Ferrari speaking from Bologna. He told me: 'Make a free passage for Gendebien. He's going like the wind in his berlinetta.' I interrupted him to tell him that he had already been through and that we had written a large OK on the blackboard. He continued: 'Then there's Collins, but he's not going to make it, his car's limping along. Taruffi's having problems too. But Von Trips is going one hundred per cent and so is De Portago.' I asked him what I should do and he replied: 'Rancati, we are Italians, aren't we?' I consulted with Carlo and we decided to carry out the 'orders' and told the drivers their actual

82

positions. Taruffi first, Von Trips second, De Portago third. Collins had stopped at Parma. All three of them went through and signalled that they had understood. Facchetti and I went back to Cremona, where we learned of the death of De Portago, his co-driver and spectators. We were numbed by the news.

A few days later, Tavoni, Ferrari's private secretary and racing manager, explained to me what had happened and that at the finish Von Trips, after having told journalists that coming in second behind Taruffi in the Mille Miglia was as good as winning it, confided that towards the end of the race he had tried several times to overtake his team-mate, who was obviously having problems, but didn't manage to.

Let us now hear what Ferrari had to say about it: 'This man, who was so fastidious in both in his technical and physical preparations before a race, had yet to win the most coveted victory, that of the Mille Miglia. Taruffi had pursued it with a touching tenacity of purpose. When it was time for the 1957 Mille Miglia, he followed my suggestion and promised his wife that if he won it he would give up racing for good. I inwardly decided that if I could help him I would. But in any case destiny was to decide it that way. Taruffi raced with great courage, struggling as an equal against wild young men like Collins, Von Trips and the other new recruits. I waited for him at Bologna. The race, which was held in bad weather conditions, was becoming dramatic. When he arrived, he told me he was suffering from mental tiredness – the severity of the contest had worn him out. What is more, his car was no longer running as well as it had been in the first part of the race. I encouraged him and said: "You must carry on because you can win." I quickly told him that Collins, who was first overall, had gone past but that he was having mechanical difficulties with his axle and so Taruffi would only have to worry about Von Trips. So Taruffi set off. As for Von Trips, I had spoken to him and the admirable young man followed my orders. Even when he saw Taruffi and caught up with him, he refrained from engaging him in a struggle that would have resulted in one of the two being eliminated. So Taruffi, in the very last of the glorious Mille Miglia races, achieved his racing-driver's dream. He kept his promise to Signora Isabella. In an interview, years later, he stated that he had engaged in a relentless struggle with Von Trips, who was trying at all costs to overtake him. By then Von Trips had been killed at Monza in the accident with Clark.'

What is the truth? I do not deny what Ferrari says, but I must also believe what Tavoni told me . . .

Let us jump ahead for a moment to 1977 and the 50th anniversary of the Mille Miglia, when the second commemorative race was organized. [In 1968, Alfa had organised an event to celebrate the 40th anniversary of the first Alfa Romeo victory]. Lancia entered three official cars, which were of course three Aurelia B20s. The pairs were: Valenzano and Roberto Bonetto (son of Felice, the lion-hearted, and an excellent journalist with *Quattroruote)*; Fabrizio Serena di Lapigio and Carlo Mariani (the first an ex-racing-driver and chairman of the *Commissione Sportiva Automobilistica Italiana* and the second a journalist with the *Messaggero* from Rome and a first-class reporter on motor races and events); and finally Taruffi and myself.

What I learnt in the three days I spent by the side of the last winner of the inimitable Mille Miglia would take up a whole book: to describe Taruffi the man, to illustrate Taruffi the driver and to discuss Taruffi the technician. An extraordinary man, with whom I strengthened an old friendship. In order to give an idea of him, it will be enough to relate the 'watch episode'. When we were getting into the car in preparation for the start he asked me what watch I had brought with me. Looking at the stopwatch he had round his neck, I confessed that I never used watches. I liked them but did not wear them. He was astonished. He put his hand in his pocket and handed me a small Tissot wrist watch. We were off and from that moment the Mille Miglia became a sort of fairy tale for me. Taruffi related anecdotes, made comments, had total recall of the points at which he had retired and the reason, gave me his opinions of other drivers, of cars and of the motorcycles with which he had started his career. I should have had a tape-recorder. Twenty years later, the crowd called out to him, acclaimed him and gave him flowers. It was an unforgettable sight. The moment came for me to ask him about his win on the 12th May 1957.

'I thought that yet again I wouldn't be able to manage it because my Ferrari was misfiring. At Bologna, Ferrari had told me not to give in. After Piacenza, Von Trips came shooting up behind me. Of course, his car was going one hundred per cent. I put all my effort into holding him off, but I wondered how long I could last, or rather, how long the car could last. As we passed Cremona, I sensed that I would have to show my young team-mate that my Ferrari was also going flat out. I told myself that if I could get to Piadena, between Cremona and Mantua, where there were a couple of bends in the middle of the town that I knew by heart and which I could drive through at full speed, then I would be able to convince Von Trips that there was nothing he could do. However, just before Piadena, he overtook me. But the bends were still to come and there among the houses, making impossible demands on both myself and the car, I managed to overtake the skilful German driver. He was then persuaded that he could no longer stop me.

When we arrived at Brescia (he had driven from Verona just like in the good old days, because we had to make up a few minutes), I took off the watch and handed it back to him. In the severe tones of an elder brother, he said to me: 'Keep it. It will remind you of me and it will remind you always to have a watch with you.' That too was Piero Taruffi, the man.

On the 18th May 1957, I received the following letter from Ferrari: 'I want to thank you for the excellent useful work you did during the Mille Miglia. I should like to know what costs you incurred at Piacenza and at Brescia so as to be able to inform the office responsible and obtain a prompt remittance. I hope you will comply with my request, since otherwise you will oblige me to keep the Mille Miglia account open and I would like to close it as soon as possible.

The 1957 Mille Miglia was an important event in Ferrari's life, both because of what happened and because of what followed. The deaths of De Portago, his co-driver Edmond Nelson Gurner and the spectators, who included many youngsters, gave rise to a lawsuit against Ferrari and against the race, which lasted for years.

Even when Ferrari made a gesture of solidarity towards the families of the victims, it served only to unleash a defamatory campaign against him.

Two weeks after the Mille Miglia, the thousand kilometre race of the Nürburgring was on the programme. It is easy to imagine the atmosphere leading up to the German race. On the Saturday morning, Von Trips asked to be allowed to try out Gendebien's berlinetta. He set out, but did not come back. The alarm went off. The driver had gone off the track in the same place where, three years before, Onofre Marimon, Fangio's pupil, had died. Von Trips was to stay in hospital for many months. The accident appears to have been caused by the way the controls in Gendebien's impressive berlinetta were arranged. The Belgian preferred to have the accelerator in the middle instead of the brake. When Von Trips had gone into the bend, he had taken his foot off the accelerator, but instead of braking, he had pressed the accelerator down again. The Ferrari clan was then faced with the problem of replacing Von Trips. The car had to be driven, or the engagement would be lost. Mino Amorotti – a Ferrari representative in racing circles, a gentleman of the old school and a man knowing all there is to know about racing – and Tavoni had to decide. At some point they noticed Olinto Morolli, a young man from Emilia who was doing well with the little OSCA. They made him a proposal and, after a little convincing, he agreed. He would take his place beside Masten Gregory in a 3000. That evening, Ferrari gave his consent. The next day, Morolli set off in Ferrari number 7. Dear Olinto received many admonitions – first and foremost, of course, was the necessity of returning to the pit. Since he did not know the circuit very well and had never driven a Ferrari before, he was under orders from the start. However, the first time the cars completed the course, he was not with them. We were beginning to give up hope and to count the minutes, when we heard a roar. It was Morolli, arriving late, but proudly signalling to the pit that he was OK. We sighed with relief and, though Gregory was complaining about his partner, we reassured him. There was no point in dramatizing things and, indeed, the pair's Ferrari was to come in tenth overall. The winner was the Aston Martin driven by Brooks and Noel Cunningham Reid, who subsequently abandoned cars to start directing film documentaries.

On the 19th July, I received a hand-written letter from Ferrari: 'Dear Rancati, Thank you for your letter. I would be very sorry to think you were not on the way to complete recovery. Patience and perseverance are required – as is faith, if you have the gift of belief. Write to me and tell me everything. I must give you one piece of bad news: Don Giulio is dead! Our dear mischievous priest was taken away in only two or three days, by a sudden poisoning of the intestines and liver. The heat, food, wine and smoking have got the better of his strong constitution. Poor Don Giulio; did he die talking of cards, tricks and money? This is the umpteenth sad episode in my life. Kindest wishes.

The last time I had seen Don Giulio was at the end of 1956, with Ferrari, Dario Zanasi, Cesare Perdisa and a dear friend from

Cremona, Delio Viti. We played cards, drank, laughed and joked with the jovial priest, who lived on the hill, amid the peace of nature. Ferrari was very fond of this priest and his words were sincere.

When I met Don Giulio for the first time at the Scuderia I realized at once of what stuff he was made. When he introduced me, Ferrari added: 'He's in Modena for a *"pratica"* [business matter]. Everyone laughed and the priest had to fend off their taunts. I did not understand the reason for so much hilarity. Later I found out that, in the Modena dialect, *'pratica'* also means mistress and Ferrari lost no opportunity to tease him in this way. The word *'pratica'* may have been the one most commonly used with him, but Don Giulio knew how to ward off the attacks and not only those of Ferrari and his friends. Don Giulio was a priest whom Pope John would have liked.

In August, Ferrari wrote to me that, following the conclusion of the inquest into the Mille Miglia, everyone would receive the 'amount entitled to him'. Then he demonstrated his concern for me and said he wanted to help me out of the long period of adversity I had been through. He kept his promise.

At the end of August, Andrea Fraschetti, the excellent designer and test-driver, died on the Modena circuit. This was another heavy blow for Ferrari.

In September, a new Ferrari made its appearance on the circuit at Modena. It had a 2400cc engine, with six cylinders in a 65° V formation, as envisaged by poor Dino. Dino, though he suffered because of his health, had always played at active part in the Ferrari company. He was interested in everything, but it was perhaps engines that interested him the most. His father wrote: 'He continued his last activity in that long, snowy winter when illness forced him to stay in bed almost all the time. Dear Jano and I spent many hours at his bedside, discussing the design of the 1500cc engine. There were many possible solutions: 4 cylinders, 6 cylinders in-line, 6 cylinders in a 65° V, 8 cylinders. I remember Dino's intensity, intelligence and attentiveness when he discussed all the notes I brought him each day from Maranello. We finally decided on the V6 engine, for reasons of mechanical efficiency and space. Thus the famous 156 came into being. It was finished in November 1956, five months after Dino's death. I had deluded myself – fathers always do – that our attentions would help him to regain his health. I had convinced myself that he was like one of my cars and so I made a table of the calorific values of the various food he had to eat – types of food that would not harm his kidneys – and I kept an up-to-date daily record of his albumins, of the specific gravity of his urine, the level of urea in his blood, of his diuresis, etc, so that I would have an indication of the progress of the disease. The sad truth was quite different: my son was gradually wasting away with progressive muscular dystrophy. He was dying of that terrible disease which no one has ever been able to understand or cure and against which there is no defence apart from genetic prophylaxis.'

Ferrari could not miss the debut of Dino's engine and I was by his side. It was the last race he would attend. From that time, he would be seen on the track at Modena and Monza for practice only. The reason for this will never be known. Ferrari said he did not want to hear his engines suffering but I think it was because, when besieged by a crowd, Ferrari did not know how to deal with either applause or criticism. He was frightened by the sea of people at races and it was better to avoid contact with them. Another possibility is that, in memory of Dino, Ferrari had decided never to attend another race. He saw the debut of the 1500, he kept faithful to the dreams of his son and now he didn't want to see any more races. Dino's creation was now out on the racing tracks and his father now kept away from them for the rest of his life.

The the 1st December, we were together in the Scuderia at Modena. Suddenly the telephone rang. It was a journalist ringing to tell Ferrari that Maserati, which had won the world championship with Fangio, had called in the receiver. It seems that it was racing itself that put the Orsi's company in difficulties. Ferrari told me the news and, looking at me, said: 'Pity it's a heavy blow for the industry – for me and for the Ferrari company too.' I have often wondered whether Ferrari was being sincere at that moment. After all, Maserati was an impressive competitor and had allowed the 'disagreeable' Fangio to win the world championship.

The 1958 Formula 1 world championship began on the 19th February in Argentina. The new regulations required fuel to contain no alcohol. Apart from Ferrari and Maserati, there was a single rear-engined Cooper in the race, driven by Stirling Moss. The Coventry Climax engine did not even come up to the maximum cylinder capacity of 2500cc. Its capacity was 1960cc with

88

174 horsepower, while the three new Ferraris driven by Musso, Collins and Hawthorn, had 285 horsepower engines. Moss won, ahead of Musso and Hawthorn. When the team returned to Modena, it fell to Amorotti to talk to Ferrari and since he was the only person who had the courage and the ability to tell the Commendatore the truth, he lost no time about it. He told Ferrari that the little Cooper (which Fangio had dubbed the 'spider') marked an important stage in the evolution of racing-cars, with its rear engine and its light weight. Amoretto prophesized that in order to win, rear-engined single-seaters would be needed in the future. 'We can manage for 1958, but next year there will be nothing we can do,' said Amorotti. Ferrari's shouts could be heard from far off, but Amorotti knew his facts and since he was a collaborator and not an employee, he had nothing to lose by sincerely stating his beliefs.

In the meantime, Carlo Chiti, from Alfa Romeo, had joined Ferrari. Chiti, who in his time had obtained a degree in aeronautical engineering, was convinced that the rear engine would be the ideal solution and he set to work. But Ferrari soon put a stop to it. He shouted to everyone that the horse should pull the cart, not push it, and his cars should have front engines. Not even Trintignant's win at Monaco in the little 2200cc Cooper from Rob Walker's stable could persuade him to change his mind. Musso and Hawthorn came in behind the Frenchman.

Therefore months of precious time were being lost at Modena. Ferrari did nothing to hasten the advent of the rear engine, in fact he found all sorts of excuses for putting it off.

In another letter to me, Ferrari wrote: 'Both Charles Markmann from the *New York post* and Gianni Marin from *Auto Italiana* have been asking for the *Ferrari Story*. Perhaps, you would be able to satisfy both these requests?' I replied that I would, and a few days later, Ferrari wrote: 'As regards the *Ferrari Story*, I would like to point out that I am not requesting you to write it, but rather I am making you a proposal, so that you can have the pleasure of seeing what you write published and also rewarded.' In other words, he did not want to get involved in the matter.

Then a journalist made a somewhat vicious attack on him. No one ever knew the reason for the attack. It appears that the journalist, who was a rather lively character – and not just with his pen – had atempted some sort of blackmail along the lines of 'I will reveal various things about your life unless you pay me to keep quiet'. Defending himself and then going on the attack in his turn became a sort of game for Ferrari. He told me that the writer of the article was not even worth the price of a postage stamp. When the journalist arrived at Modena, Ferrari showed him an immense dossier, of which he was the subject, and which he inspected. Nothing was missing; it was all there. The journalist left with his tail between his legs.

On the 6th July the French Grand Prix took place. Hawthorn and Musso marked up the best times in their Ferraris, but Musso, a member of the 'Ferrari Spring' squad, died in the race. It seems that the Roman driver had pushed a bit too hard in an attempt to win at all costs. The prizes on offer at Reims were particularly large and a win would have helped poor Luigi to get out of a worrying situation. Musso's death would weigh particularly heavily on Enzo Ferrari. Manual Fangio, in a Maserati, also raced at Reims and he came in fourth. After the Grand Prix, he announced that he was giving up racing. He was 47 years old and his decision confirmed that he was, above all, a thinking person. A great racing-driver – and a man who has been fully described in Ferrari's memoirs – thus left the scene.

At the Nürburgring, only a short time after Musso's death, Peter Collins was killed at the wheel of a Ferrari. On the day Tony Brooks achieved another win in the green Vanwall, the Italian team lost a great racing-driver. Early in February 1957, someone from the Ferrari company had written to me: 'If you want an example of a racing-driver who is serious, disciplined and able, you need only mention Collins. When you talk about the best drivers in the world, don't stop at Fangio and Moss, include Collins.' When a racing-driver dies, people always want to know why it happened. I remember that after the German Grand Prix, which was held on the formidable Nürburgring, someone unearthed a rather nasty story. According to this version, Hawthorn had practically forced his team-mate off the track, with the consequences we all know. The reason for this was that an intoxicating passion had blossomed between the blonde Mike and Louise, Collins' wife.

Ferrari wrote: 'This woman, Louise, was one of those typical female visitors to the pits that we fleetingly remembered. That tour in Florida was decisive for Collins. The American woman fascinated him and won his heart. Peter telephoned her father and married her. Collins continued to be an enthusiastic, skilful and outstanding driver, but his cheerful character was undermined and he became nervous. His friends whispered to one another that the American woman was preventing him from sleeping. My last memory of him is when I shook his hand before he left for the Nürburgring. I looked at him and I was overwhelmed by a feeling of great sadness. When I got back to my office I wondered whether this was a premonition.'

Meanwhile, Hawthorn continued his fight for the world title. He was engaged in a fascinating struggle with Moss.

Mike's Ferrari was in tip-top condition, but the Englishman, a brave and very capable driver, considered that the braking system could be improved. He wanted to have disc brakes fitted for the Italian Grand Prix. At Modena, they complied with his wishes. Ferrari had always said that drum brakes were sufficient but he had to give way to this new system. In fact, he adopted disc brakes on all his cars in the following year.

With his second place at Monza and his second place at Casablanca in the Moroccan Grand Prix, Hawthorn became world champion. He was 29 years old. He had seen his dreams come true and he decided to retire. He asked Ferrari for the single-seater which had enabled him to become world champion.

In January 1959, he too was killed, but this time in a road accident. The tragedy seems to have been caused by rain and by the speed with which Mike was driving a Jaguar in an attempt to avoid being overtaken by a friend in a Mercedes. He was a strange character; he would always talk to Italian journalists in English, even though he knew our language. However, this has always been a habit (let's call it that) amongst British racing-drivers.

Let us return to October 1958, when *La Civiltà Cattolica* published an article by Father Leonardo Azzollini entitled: *Una inutile strage: le gare automobilistiche di velocità* ['The unnecessary slaughter of high-speed motor-racing']. The text was inspired by an article published on the 9th July in the *Osservatore Romano*, in which Ferrari was described as a Saturn who devoured his own sons. Here is an extract from this attack: 'He is a modern-day Saturn. Having become a captain of industry, he continues to devour his own sons. The myth has unfortunately been reflected in reality. Luigi Musso is the latest of his victims and his death has brought about the usual expressions of mourning and regret, which have only one serious fault – that nothing is learned from their frequent recurrence, that the message underlying all this heartbroken stupor is going unnoticed, the message that cries out "enough!" ' This article had been published a few days after Musso's death. In October, *La Civiltà Cattolica* called for an end to motor-racing. One afternoon, Ferrari arrived at the Scuderia with the Jesuits' publication in his hand. He was feeling very bitter and did not know what to do. I told him that I had a good Jesuit friend in Parma, whom I had known and visited in 1951 when I had been working with *La Gazetta di Parma* for a few months. I offered to telephone him and ask for his advice, which I did.

Some days later, I learned that Father Azzollinin would be coming to Modena to meet Ferrari. This he duly did.

The man from Maranello spent a long time with the Jesuit priest. He managed to demonstrate to him that he could not be blamed. Who knows what words and images he came out with. In March 1959, Father Azzollini wrote in *La Civiltà Cattolica:* 'Finally, it is our opinion that the responsibility for races should be borne exclusively and entirely by the organizers and by those in public office. Car-makers such as Ferrari do not fall into either category.'

This was quite a volte-face. Either Father Azzollini wrote his October attack on motor-racing without knowing the facts, or Ferrari had once again been able to use his incomparable powers of persuasion to influence him. What mattered was that the Jesuits' organ had changed its mind. Here was yet another example of sweet revenge in the Ferrari story.

The races of 1959 proved that Mino Amorotti had been right. The world title was won for the first time by the Australian driver, Jack Brabham, in the Cooper.

Of the eight world championship contests, Tony Brooks won two for Ferrari, one in France and one in Germany. The latter was not held at the Nürburgring, but on the fast Avus track. In practice, the French driver, Jean Behra, was killed in a Porsche. He was among the most easy-going drivers of the fifties and was not only charming, but a joker too. In a previous accident, he had lost an ear which was replaced with a plastic one. If he found himself with people who did not know of his 'disability', he would look them in the eye, put his hand to his ear and very gradually turn it as if he was unscrewing it and taking if off! Imagine the reaction . . .! Behra could certainly be difficult, and having started the season with Ferrari, he soon quarrelled with Romolo Tavoni and left. This is why when he was at the Avus on the 1st August he was in a Porsche.

On the 16th Sepember, Ferrari wrote to me: 'I have received your kind letter. It is a situation which *must* touch rock bottom. We are near that point and later we will start again from zero. That is how I see it. best wishes.'

He was obviously referring to the year's defeats.

On the 2nd November, I received another letter in which Ferrari told me that he had not gone to Monza for practice 'for reasons that are to be found in the deal I have clinched in Bologna regarding the acquisition of Ford of Italy from Signor Paradise, whose speech you sent me.' The speech referred to was the one made at the *Salone di Torino* [Turin Motor Show] by the chairman of Ford of Italy, which had caused a stir because of its controversial and threatening tone. I had immediately sent Ferrari a copy.

12

The Ford affair and the degree from the University of Bologna

Two things arose from the Ford affair: the degree in engineering and the negotiations which would begin, years later, over the acquisition of Ferrari by the great American company.

The acquisition by Ferrari of Ford's office in Bologna was above all a valuable public relations coup. The affair was proposed to Ferrari by Cesare Perdisa, the ex-racing-driver and shrewd bargainer. The man from Maranello realized immediately the prestige involved in the acquisition of the building – a now celebrated, but still small, member of the car industry was buying the Italian headquarters of the second biggest car-maker in the world. Ferrari brought the negotiations to a successful conclusion.

The news spread throughout Italy and the world and many people thought that this could mean that Ferrari intended to leave Modena and Maranello and move to Bologna. He let people say and write what they wanted without comment. It was then that Professor Morandi, the envoy of the Rector of the University of Bologna, came to Ferrari to offer him the degree. Ferrari did not let the opportunity slip by, and quickly offered the university a sum of money for research or any other purpose. Professor Morandi returned to Bologna greatly touched.

A little later, Ferrari sold the building to a bank, 'earning us a few million', as Perdisa said. But by then the degree had already been awarded.

Apart from this conquest, Ferrari began a dialogue with Ford which much, much later led to negotiations to cede the Ferrari company to the heirs of the great Henry I. We will see later that this was no doubt one of the events that revealed the most about Enzo Ferrari's qualities.

Together with the degree and the opening of discussions with the Americans, Ferrari also got people talking about his company because of the small car he had decided to have designed and marketed. This was the little 850, the manufacture of which was opposed by almost everyone at Maranello, especially Gardini, the factory's sales manager, who said: 'Ferrari should make cars for rich people, not little GT's'. But he went ahead and built it, even exhibited at some shows, then sold it and of course made a profit. At that time the little 850 perhaps gave him the chance to annoy someone. It was indisputable that a 'Ferrarina' on the market would aggravate other manufacturers. Even though it was expensive, the little car from Maranello could be dangerous for the large factories that made small-engined GT cars.

Some years later, when I was alone with Ferrari one evening at Maranello, he showed me a wonderful silver GT. Even though it was half covered by a tarpaulin, I could make out the purity of its outline and its aggressiveness. I asked whether it was a new Ferrari. He answered without really telling me anything and I thought I had discovered that it was a prototype prepared by Ferrari for Innocenti – 6-cylinder engine, 1600cc. I seem to remember that later Alfa Romeo made it plain that Innocenti did not put such cars on the market. All things must end, but Ferrari started a period of consultation with Innocenti, which would last for some time.

'On the 5th February 1960, he wrote to me: 'Dear Rancati, I complied with your friendly requests and, having spoken for 1 minute 16 seconds, I heard just 37 seconds on the TV. Your friendship justifies this and other things besides and I hope to see you soon and not just on the television screen.' What a character he was, this Ferrari! I had not noticed that, while I was interviewing him, he was timing the proceedings. No doubt he is not the only person in the automobile world to do so.

On the 7th April, my good friend and a very capable investigative journalist, Mario Morselli – who was to die in October 1976 – communicated the following from Modena: 'Following the proposal by the eminent Professor Dore, head of the Faculty of Engineering at the University of Bologna, the faculty unanimously decided to seek the approval of the minister of education for the bestowal of an honorary degree in mechanical engineering to the Cavaliere del lavoro, Enzo Ferrari. The minister, Signor Medici, has given his authorization and so, in the next few days, the manufacturer from Modena – whose technical activity has won great esteem for our country in the eyes of the world – will collect his academic qualification in the university.'

To my telegram of congratulations, Ferrari replied: 'Dear Rancati. Among the many congratulations I have received, the ones from my friend Gino are the most welcome. See you soon and best wishes.'

Thus the deed was done and Ferrari felt very gratified, though he did not show it. The first result of the acquisition of the Ford building had been very satisfying.

On the 29th May, the 19th Monaco Grand Prix was held. As well as the two Dino 246's driven by Phil Hill and Von Trips, Ferrari entered the new rear-engined single-seater and entrusted it to Richie Ginther. So even the manufacturer from Maranello was at last convinced! In the trials, Von Trips achieved 1 minute 38.3 seconds and Hill and Ginther both 1 minute 38.6 seconds.

Hill came in third and Ginther sixth, showing that having the 'horse behind the cart' was the right decision.

In June, there were changes at the Ferrari company. The Commendatore mentioned to me that he had 'plunged into a *Societa per Azioni* [joint stock company]' SEFAC. The move was made for financial reasons and also to provide Ferrari with some cover from the consequences of racing accidents. It should be remembered that the inquest into the 1957 Mille Miglia tragedy was still in progress.

On the 22nd July, a communique arrived. The text was as follows: 'Dear Sir, We have pleasure in informing you that on the 23rd May last there was formed – by a deed of the same date given to Dr Giuliano Cuoghi of Modena, no. 20119/12231, the limited company called "*Societa Esercizio Fabbriche Automobili e Corse – S.E.F.A.C.*". The board of directors consists of Prince Carlo Caracciolo, Dott. Ugo Colombo, Cav. del Lavoro Giovanni Battista Farina, Dott. Ing. Enzo Ferrari, Dott. Ing. Michel Paul-Cavallier. The object of the company is the construction of Ferrari cars and the participation in sporting competitions, taking over from the *Auto Costruzioni* Ferrari firm, whose suspension has been arranged for the end of the present month.'

Ferrari therefore now had associates, but he was still in control. Some people immediately noticed that S.E.F.A.C. could also stand for *'Sempre Enzo Ferrari Anche Cambiando'* ['Still Enzo Ferrari Although Changing']! This was quite accidental, but if Ferrari had done it on purpose, it would have been another of his coups, about which he could have laughed with his friends. Even though he had associates (in a manner of speaking), Ferrari liked to say: 'Who could I leave the Ferrari company to? To a trust of American millionaires? If I carry on, in the midst of such incomprehension, in the midst of so many enemies within and without, if I fight like an old and tired lion who roars more than he lashes out, I do it only for the three hundred families of my workers.' Being melodramatic came naturally to him.

But it should be said that Ferrari was too closely involved with his factory not to be also involved with the people that worked with him. He also knew that without them he could go no further. There were many who left the factory and continued to carry out some task or other for the Commendatore. Until a few years ago, he used to invite all his staff to lunch once a year, on the day of the press conference. But at that time his 'forces' were fewer in number and room could be found for the splendid meal. Then the custom declined.

The day of the degree ceremony came and the 850 plan went ahead. In August, I received two lines: 'Dear Signor Gino, The 854 will soon change its name and you may be the first to be privileged to try out the car with its new name.'

'The company was going well. There were 320 staff and the production was five cars a week.

On the 8th October, I received another letter: 'Dear Signor Gino, Thank you for your letter of the 3rd October. The pipe that took the hydraulic fluid to one of the brake calipers was indeed cracked, causing all the fluid in the brake master cylinder to leak away. This does not mean that the Count was competing sensibly, because if he had pushed ahead right from the start, as the car was able to do, instead of waiting till the 72nd lap to check its actual capabilities, he would have built up a sufficient margin to protect him from the regrettable trouble 12 laps from the end.'

I do not remember which race this letter was referring to but I believe that when Ferrari says the 'Count', he means Von Trips.

Nuvolari, oh, Nuvolari . . .

On the 10th December there was the usual end-of-year meeting and I was present, even though it was restricted to Ferrari's intimates. In the evening I was in the Scuderia with an engineer when I received a telephone call from the television news people in Milan telling me that on the following day I had to go to Monza for the last race of the season, the Coppa Carri. I set off and on that beautiful sunny day I discovered . . .Giancarlo Baghetti. I already knew him, having seen him several times in races, but what he did that day with his Lancia Dagrada no. 102 – he even won – encouraged me to speak to Ferrari about him. On Monday 11th December, I wrote to Ferrari saying that perhaps the only young Italian driver who could be of any use to him was Giancarlo Baghetti. I liked his coolness, his way of driving and even his aggressiveness, which was so unexpected in a young man who appeared so mild and serene.

13

Tazio Nuvolari - an obsession

Some time, after my letter about Baghetti was received, Ferrari informed me that he was going to entrust one of his formula 1 single-seaters to *FISA (Federazione Italiana Scuderie Automobilistiche)* [Italian Federation of Motor-racing Stables], whose factotum was a great motor racing enthusiast. This was Eugenio Dragoni, who would later become the Ferrari racing manager. As for Baghetti, for months he walked around with the first letter he had received from Ferrari in his pocket and every now and then would read it to himself or to anyone else who would listen. Then Ferrari informed me that, as well as Baghetti, he had decided to take on Dragoni. He said: 'You will be pleased – first the driver, then the racing manager, and both of them your friends.' Years later, Baghetti, who is now a good photographer, would say that it was Dragoni who took him to the Ferrari company, whereas the opposite is true. A few days before the Siracusa Grand Prix, I interviewed Baghetti and Bandini (who was racing for the *Scuderia Centro Sud)* for the television news. I knew that these two young men had much to say and that they were capable of bringing great satisfaction to Italian motor-racing. The Grand Prix was set for the 25th April and in the middle of that afternoon, one of the television news secretaries handed me the phone without saying who was on the line. I just had time to say 'hello', when I heard a voice say: 'He's beaten the lot of them'. It was Ferrari telling me that Baghetti had won the race. I was very pleased and Baghetti did not let me down in the French Grand Prix either. This was held at Reims in July and Baghetti won it with a flying finish in which both his great ability and his fierce determination were apparent.

Perhaps the driver Ferrari had been looking for had been found? Perhaps here was a promising young champion like Achille Varzi. Ferrari did not praise Baghetti too much, but it was clear that he was satisfied, however Ferrari was worried that the young driver's performances might just be a flash in the pan.

Unfortunately, little by little, Baghetti started to loose his shine. At the end of the year, I was having dinner with Ferrari and Jano. The conversation came round to Baghetti, and Ferrari attacked him severely. I replied that his words were perhaps a little too harsh and that, when it came down to it, young Baghetti had won him some races and even the French Grand Prix. Jano told me not to make Ferrari get worked up; if I stayed quiet, he would get over it. It was not a successful evening.

Ferrari thought he had discovered what Baghetti was really like. Perhaps he had hoped for too much and he was now left with a young man who, in his opinion, was not prepared to sacrifice everything to racing, racing in a Ferrari in particular. The following year, when Bandini had also become one of his drivers (and both he and Baghetti were working as test-drivers), Ferrari gave me a rather negative opinion of the two of them. He preferred Bandini to Baghetti, because he was mechanically-minded, because he was not nice in the same way as Baghetti was and because he was more open. I wrote in *Il Giorno* that the difference between Baghetti and Bandini was that the latter was prepared to die for Ferrari, but not the former. And that, unfortunately, is what happened . . .

When Ferrari evaluated a driver he inevitably compared him to Nuvolari. He would look back at the great Tazio and was certain that no one could match him. Then, one day we were at Monza watching Richie Ginther – the small, freckled American driver who is now an archaeologist – as he climbed into his car. Ferrari said: 'He's like Nuvolari, there's no doubt about it. And he goes fast.' But Ginther was also to disappoint him, as did many others. When Ginther left Maranello, Ferrari said angrily: 'And when he came to Maranello he was all in rags!'

He searched everywhere and had numerous names suggested to him, but was not able to find the right man. His search was also hindered because he no longer went to races and could not know everything that was happening.

Ferrari had discovered Guy Moll. About this Algerian driver, he wrote: 'In the 1934 Monte Carlo Grand Prix, Varzi was beaten by a beginner. He was called Guy Moll and he had the potential to be one of the greatest racing-car aces that have ever existed. Sadly, he was to be a shooting star, though an unforgettable one. In August of the same year, he was killed on the Pescara circuit. He was overtaking Henne's Mercedes on the straight stretch of road leading to Montesilvano. There was a skid, probably caused by a collision, and Moll went off the road and died instantly. Moll was not the first foreign driver in my stable, but he was undoubtedly the first sensational driver. He had a Spanish mother and a French father, who had emigrated to Algeria, where he was born. I do not know whether this mixture of nationalities and environments helped to turn the young man into a prodigy but, in my opinion, he was in any case the only racing-driver worthy of being placed side by side with Nuvolari, along with Moss. He had a strange mental affinity with Nuvolari and the same aggressive spirit, the same self-confidence at the wheel, the same faith when facing great risks.

There he goes again! Nuvolari was an obsession. Ferrari did not discover anyone after Moll, at least not anyone who could have resembled a new 'red devil', as they called Nuvolari in Britain. He came close to getting Stirling Moss, but the great English driver, who never managed to become world champion (Villoresi maintained that the fact that Moss had to prove 'officially' that he was the best only ended up irritating him), seriously injured himself on the Easter Monday of 1962 at Goodwood and had to give up serious racing. So Ferrari, who was desperately searching for a successor to Nuvolari, had to give up. This was quite a blow for him.

A friend of mine told me that when Nuvolari and Varzi saw Moll racing, they said they would have to start collecting money for a wreath, because he would not last long. They were right.

Mario Andretti, who raced both in Formula 1 and in sports cars, was also once a member of the Ferrari team. Ferrari described him one day as 'possibly the Nuvolari of the 1970s'. But if he had heard what the little driver from Trieste said – 'The finest day in my life was a day in April 1964, when I became an American citizen' – he would perhaps never have entrusted one of his racing cars to him. Ferrari was a patriotic Italian. He always looked for Italian drivers, and would rather not look abroad, because a win by a Ferrari in the hands of an Italian was worth twice as much. Later, when he found that if an Italian driver was killed, the public outcry was so great and he would be the subject of so many unbearable attacks, he had to change his stance and began to say that he could no longer take on Italian drivers.

I think that Ferrari did not rate his drivers' professionalism very highly. He did not believe in their total love for the racing-car and was always afraid that they did not know how to push the accelerator to the floor when necessary. When I went to Maranello just before Christmas in 1976. I told him that Vittorio Brambilla had given me a message – he wanted to know why he would not give him a Ferrari. Vittorio had said: Ferrari must win the Championship now, and I'm not too old. If Ferrari wants to make me wait for years then of course I will be too old.' I repeated the message to Ferrari but he just shrugged his shoulders and didn't say a word.

I am convinced that if he had not been afraid that Brambilla would have an accident, he would have done all he could to give him a Ferrari. Vittorio was a modest, brave man and completely dedicated to the car he had always dreamed of. But what if Ferrari gave him a car and something happened?

One foggy evening I was with Romolo Tavoni outside the Scuderia Ferrari when we happened to meet Mr Martin, the racing man from Shell. Martin told us he had come to see Ferrari to offer him John Surtees, the 'son of the wind' motorcyclist but the Commendatore had turned him down. He had never been a great fan of the English and did not really believe in Surtees' ability. But the following year Shell insisted: 'Ferrari says he has the cars but no drivers, so we are giving him an exceptional driver.' Surtees became world champion in 1964, but his time at Ferrari's was never untroubled.

When Lodovico Scarfiotti came to Modena to try out a Ferrari, he was given to me to look after. We went to Fini's to eat, but Scarfiotti was preoccupied because his wife's first baby was overdue. All I could do was to encourage him and tell him that on the next morning he should drive smoothly, without overdoing things. On the following day there was rain and fog at the *aerautodromo* – it was the worst possible day for getting abroad a Ferrari car to show one's abilities. There were two sports cars waiting, a 2000 and a 3000. I was in the pit with Ferrari and a few others: we watched Scarfiotti start slowly, then become increasingly confident. Afterwards, as we were going back to the Scuderia, Ferrari told me that he had liked the young man better in the 3000 than in the 2000. This was a positive opinion, but he also told me that he did not know how to get Lodovico racing because the driver's father had expressed his fear of his son motor racing . . .

Ferrari later engaged the great Stewart who raced one of his sports cars, but never got in a formula 1 car, and it was precisely for the single-seater that Ferrari needed an ace.

When Dan Gurney, the ex-marine, arrived at Modena, Tavoni and I went to Real Fini to meet him: we found a giant. He would prove an excellent driver for Ferrari, but unfortunately not excellent enough.

The 1960 Le Mans 24 Hour Race was won by a Ferrari driven by two Belgians – Olivier Gendebien and Paul Frère, the latter a journalist and racing driver. Some time later I asked Paul whether Ferrari had sent any message of congratulations or thanks after the win. 'No,' he replied. 'I was the one who was asking a favour of him. I did so want to have the steering wheel of the Ferrari with which Oliver and I won the race. When the wheel arrived, I saw Signor Ferrari's signature engraved on one of the spokes.'

All of these men were good drivers: people who won races, but they were a far cry from Nuvolari. When Ferrari did find the right man, he reminded him, unfortunately, of Achille Varzi. That is how Ferrari described Niki Lauda to me, but he went on to say that the Austrian had one advantage over the great Achille – he was more technical and knew more about mechanics.

Niki was brought to him by Regazzoni. In 1973, when the man from Ticino was with BRM, Ferrari approached him about a possible return to the Cavallino. Clay had already raced for the Cavallino in 1969, 1970, 1971 and 1972. Then, being a little too determined and having destroyed quite a few cars in his desire to go faster and faster, he left.

But Ferrari liked Clay, who reminded him in his own way of the courage of Nuvolari, and asked him back. At Maranello, they asked Clay his opinion of the Frenchman Jarier.

Clay realized that they would like him with Jarier in 1974, so he spoke frankly: 'Ferrari, if you are looking for another young man as well as me, I know someone. He's Austrian and his name is Niki Lauda. He's with me at BRM. I think he's the right man.' And so it happened.

Later Clay would discover that Lauda was faster than he was and would see him win the world championship. Ferrari took a liking to Niki because the Austrian reminded him of when he was young and shy. 'Just like me.'

In 1976, at the end of the live television report from the Western United States Grand Prix, Luca Montezemolo, who had helped me in my work, called Maranello to get Ferrari's opinion on the race and the programme. Then he handed me the receiver. Ferrari said to me in sarcastic tones: 'What a good lie by Regazzoni, saying he brought me Lauda. A very imaginative lie.'

It would not have been appropriate to object and anyway I could understand the Grand Old Man. He had been chasing after an impressive driver for years and, now that he had one, he wanted to believe that he himself had made the discovery. In other words, Lauda was his creation and even if he did not remind him of Nuvolari, he was one of the best drivers he had ever had. Lauda was serious, professional and completely dedicated to racing and to the preparation of the cars. When he was practising on the track at Fiorano, he didn't want to stop, even when the mechanics pointed out to him that it was dark. He would say: 'There's light enough for another two or three laps, then we can go home.'

When he unexpectedly returned to racing after the horrific accident at the Nürburgring in 1976, the practices for the Italian Grand Prix at Monza were arranged for 11 o'clock on the Sunday morning. Lauda was at his post ten minutes early, because he wanted to check something. Ermanno Cuoghi, the faithful head mechanic, arrived 30 seconds late. Lauda showed him his watch and Cuoghi tried to apologize, even though he was less than a minute late. But Lauda replied: 'In my condition, I could easily have rested for a little longer, but my duty is to be punctual even when I don't feel like it.' He shot off in the Ferrari for another practice before the race. He would surprise everyone by achieving an impressive fourth place.

Nevertheless, before the Nürburgring, when the Ferrari cars no longer seemed as unbeatable as at the start of the season, Ferrari found a way of slipping into his conversation the idea that both the drivers, Lauda and Regazzoni, were perhaps no longer working as before. It was only a very slight reproach, but he made it nevertheless. He had forgotten about misfortunes Lauda had had, with the fall from a tractor and the sadness of his wife's miscarriage.

It would be interesting to know how Lauda reacted to Ferrari's attitude. Regazzoni would have smiled at the criticism, but not the young Austrian. Definitely not.

Then the Nürburgring accident happened and Ferrari must certainly have gone through a terrible time. Apart from the upset at what happened to Niki, the possibility arose that he would be without the great driver in the future. The people from the Scuderia started to think about a replacement: they saw Scheckter, then Reutemann. But when Lauda, who had made a quick recovery, discovered this interest in other drivers, he decided to do something about it – 'Ferrari is looking for other people, but he hasn't finished with me yet' – and he announced that he would be in one of the Ferraris at Monza. Lauda was as good as his word: Ferrari must have appreciated such a temperament. What other driver would have done the same? Lauda may have been racing for himself, but he was also racing for the Ferrari company: he was the right man for Ferrari to have.

One day I told Ferrari that I had met one of his ex-drivers, Ickx, on the track at Hockenheim and that he had spoken enthusiastically about the 'Commendatore'. He replied brusquely: 'He would have done better to get down to work when he was with me. I used to have to get down on my knees to make him test-drive a car. It's a bit late to speak well of me now.'

There is no doubt that Ferrari always felt his drivers were indebted to him. There is also another consideration which he would never acknowledge – he would not like it if the merits of a driver were considered greater than those of the Ferrari he was driving. He was the maker of the best racing cars in the world and his drivers were lucky to be entrusted with these gems.

At the end of the year, Clay left Ferrari. Perhaps he was paying fot the collision with Lauda in the British Grand Prix, perhaps for something else. Regazzoni's exuberance meant that he was always living dangerously.

Ferrari said: 'Regazzoni has been racing just for himself recently. I did that too, when I used to race.' But now he was the boss. Regazzoni accused Ferrari of never going to races and of having to believe what others told him.

Relations between the drivers of the same stable are often tense. Regazzoni had difficulty in putting up with the fact that young Niki had started to beat him; and the Austrian driver never denied that he considered his team mate or mates to be his competitors along with everyone else. Nevertheless, drivers always pretend to get along amongst themselves, and those that help them to race also contribute to this impression of calmness.

This is why I was so surprised by a statement from Sante Ghedini, Ferrari's racing manager, in early January 1977. Ghedini had just arrived at Buenos Aires for the Argentinian Grand Prix. He said: 'Lauda and Reutemann both start the season as equals. There is no first driver and no second driver. In this team, the order of priority and of support for one or the other will be established according to the circumstances. If Reutemann suddenly starts to win a lot of points, we pay him the most attention. If the opposite is true, we support Lauda.'

Ghedini may have actually uttered these words, but I would like to bet that Ferrari made him learn them by heart before he left for South America. The style is certainly that of the boss. I must say that this statement surprised me. How can people say such things? Was Lauda already to be thrown out? Would they really not want to allow him an appeal? And what did he mean by supporting one or the other? Each single-seater has its own equipment and men.

Many people have written, and it is true, that Ferrari always tried to set his drivers one against another, except when they were called Nuvolari or Varzi. However, this time I thought he was going too far. Before struggling against Hunt and everyone else, Reutemann and Lauda now had to struggle against one another in order to settle an unnecessary and dangerous order of supremacy within Ferrari.

Various denials and soothing noises would later be made, but they would come too late.

Poor Niki. I have not spoken to him for a long time but, if I could speak to him, I would tell him that the heart of this romantic old car-racing enthusiast is with him and my support is still strong.

I said that I have not spoken to Lauda for a long time. In fact, I tried to do so when Niki went home after the Nürburgring accident. I called Gozzi and asked him for the number. He replied: 'I've got his old number but not the number of his new house. I can't help you.' Such methods are often used in Ferrari circles. It was not that Gozzi did not give me the number because he was worried I might disturb Lauda, it was more to avoid granting a reasonable request.

14

Ferrari accused ~ and acquitted

We have seen how in 1964 Ferrari's single-seaters raced in America painted white and blue and how the Formula Uno aperitif was drunk at Ferrari's table during that period. It is perhaps appropriate to say that this gesture is a typical example of Ferrari's way of dealing with the world. In other words, he uses threats – 'I am stopping'/'I am going away'/'I am tired of Italy'.

Once he even said that he wanted to move to Switzerland. Then, when his son died, he told me that he would only continue racing until the end of the year, then give up (this example at least was understandable). Another time he threatened to give it all up and to go away, but turned up punctually the next day.

At the reception for the debut of the GT250 2 + 2, an event which cost five and half million lire (Ferrari had by then adopted the practice of launching his models in a fashionable setting, where he would enjoy fascinating the beautiful women – another example of him getting his own back), he said that he intended to retire and that his decision should be considered 'definitive and irrevocable'.

On a sultry afternoon in June 1961, I was at Maranello. I was watching the cars that were going to compete in the Le Mans 24 hour race being loaded on to a lorry.

A friend of mine came up behind me and whispered: 'You'd better prepare yourself. Tonight you are going to meet Piero and his mother.' I managed to control my surprise and not to turn around.

I had known about this boy for some time. He had been born on the 22nd May 1945 and was called Piero Lardi, his mother's surname, but he *was* Ferrari's son.

Around eight in the evening, Ferrari came out of his office. The grey 250 GT was waiting in the courtyard. I think that the number plate, which was five numbers long, started with a 5 and had a 3, a 0 and an 8 in it. Peppino, the chauffeur, was ready and the door was already open. Ferrari said: 'Peppino, I'm going in Gino's car. I want to see what his driving's like. You follow us.'

I got into my Fiat 1300 and Ferrari sat next to me. The gate was open. I waited for instructions. 'Turn left, then at Maranello go straight towards Vignola.' It was the road we had gone along almost a year before on the day of the degree ceremony.

Outside Maranello, he said: 'We are going to see a boy who lives with his mother. They have a farm where they grow cherries and plums. Turn right, straight on, turn left, slowly, there's a sharp bend, go on.'

The short, but seemingly never-ending trip brought us to a beautiful house with red brick walls. No sooner had we opened the car doors than Piero came running up with a shrill: 'Papa, hello papa.' I was amazed. The similarity of the boy with the photographs I had seen of his father as a young man was astounding. He was an exact copy; 'pantographed', as we used to say. Piero had had his sixteenth birthday the year before.

His mother arrived. She was a real lady – in her features, her demeanour and her simple elegance. She must have been about 50 years old. I said hello to her and I immediately felt a deep sympathy for this woman who had for some time been living in the shadow of a man to whom she had given a child.

I said to myself: 'This is Ferrari's real wife. What a couple. Both of them tall, she much milder than he, they are very well suited.'

They were linked by this son, who for signora Lina was the mark of a very painful destiny. It must have been a difficult relationship to live with.

She had made us an exquisite dinner, accompanied by a rosé Lambrusco that was as refreshing as spring water.

We chatted about this and that, about the heat, the fruit and how good it was. I have never – before or since – tasted such cherries as signora Lina's.

I looked at the mother and at her son and I decided that my 'mission' would be to persuade Ferrari to give his name to the boy. It was to be a very hard battle. Ferrari shouted at me that when Piero was born he had put a lot of money in the bank for him and that the only Ferrari after him had been Dino. It was a battle that I lost, though I fought with all my strength. Against me, against us, was Laura, Ferrari's legitimate wife and Dino's mother.

Ferrari later went as far as leaving home, to live in the Palace Hotel and offering his wife whatever she wanted if he could only give his name to the boy. She did not budge an inch. A story went round at Modena that Ferrari had offered his wife one thousand million lire just to be able to give his name to the boy and that she had accepted. The sum was put into the bank, but then she had second thoughts and Ferrari took the money back. Someone called it the 'elastic thousand million lira.'

Poor Laura, she also deserved a great deal of pity. One day she asked me if I was going to see my parents in Cremona that evening. I replied that I was. A little later she gave me a shoebox full of apples and told me: 'Rancati, these are for your mother.' My mother was touched. But then she was dismayed to find that under the top layer of beautiful fruits was a layer of almost rotten apples . . .

After the first meeting there were frequent dinners with Lina in her flat in Modena. We never talked of the argument that was raging, but it can easily be understood that Piero's mother latched on to me. Then, suddenly, she and Piero disappeared: Ferrari no longer let me see them. I could not even telephone to say 'hello'. I understood and gave up: Ferrari had said no.

I did see Piero's mother again, years later at Monza during practice for an Italian Grand Prix. I was amongst the red single-seaters and she was above the pits. We exchanged a brief greeting. When Piero joined the Ferrari company I would see him frequently. He always ate with his father and with the latter's guests, to whom he was on rare occasions quickly introduced. Although he still looked very similar to Ferrari, some people would wonder who the quiet young man was . . . until he turned to Ferrari and called him 'papa'.

Many times I wanted to ask how he felt about the memory of Dino – who was so often mentioned by his father, even in his presence – but I never had the nerve. I would meet him, ask after his mother, tell him to give her my regards and then I would stop.

After Laura's death on the 27th February 1978, Ferrari performed the long-awaited act – he recognized Piero, who would thereafter be called Lardi Ferrari. I remembered how, years ago, Dr

Alvaro Magnoni (Piero's physician) and I had devised a plan – a legal one, naturally – to have the name Piero Lardi Ferrari written in the birth registry, so long as his father agreed. Then his name would have become Piero Ferrari Lardi and finally the name Lardi would disappear. We thought we could go ahead, but his father firmly advised us against it.

Although I did not feel able to ask Piero about Dino, other people did. He would reply: 'I never knew Dino' but I have never felt I was a victim of his memory or of the pain that my father has always felt because of his death. And I would not be being sincere if I did not say that when I was recognized I experienced a great deal of emotion.'

Piero is now a man, with a family of his own, but his father's obsession with Dino's memory must have left a mark on him.

When the hearings about the 1957 Mille Miglia accident started, Ferrari said: 'Why should I continue with an activity whose only reward is to be considered a murderer? As from the 1st July, I am retiring.'

On the 26th July, Bonafini, the examining magistrate at the Court of Mantua found that 'Ferrari should immediately be acquitted of the charge brought against him' and ordered that all the evidence seized from him should be returned.

Among other things, the judgement said: '. . . guilt consisted of having used on the cars from his "Scuderia" that were entered in the 24th Mille Miglia, and in particular on the car driven by Alfonso Cabeza de Vaca the Marquis De Portago, racing number 531, number plate BO 81825, tyres made by the "Englebert" company from Liège, Belgium. Tyres which, because of their characteristics of construction and preparation (tread about 8mm thick and inflated to 2.5kg/cm2) were not suited to the performance of the cars. Cars which at full engine speed could reach speeds of at least 280kph, whereas these tyres allowed a maximum of 220kph, and, because of the overheating resulting from excessive inflation, causing the central part of the tread to become detached and subsequently the whole tyre to burst, with the result that the car skidded, occasioning the death of . . .'

And again: '. . . on the sides of the road, beyond the grass verge and on the edges of the ditches running parallel to the layer of asphalt, were numerous people, most of them local and inhabiting the cottages looking out on the Provinciale Bresciana road. The Mille Miglia, a very popular contest, had attracted them and they came to watch the exciting final stage – in fact only a little more than 30 kilometres separated the said locality from the finishing line at Brescia. Suddenly a tearing explosion was heard and De Portago's car, which was travelling at the speed described above, skidded frighteningly, leaving traces of rubber, towards the left for more than 65 metres until it reached the edge of the road. From there, it continued along the excavated verge (still on the left side, in the Mantua-Brescia direction) for another 26 metres, until it hit a stone post, which was literally sliced through by the force of the car. After this it uprooted a telegraph pole and hit another stone post and, still possessing considerable kinetic energy, continued along the ditch, brushing, smashing and scraping various plants, re-emerged on to the road, which it crossed diagonally, and finally came to rest in the ditch on the right-hand side. The ditch contained water to a depth of about 65cm; in all, the car had gone more than 200 metres from the place of the tyre burst. From that place to the place it stopped, the road, the grass verge and the ditches were strewn with fragments of the car's body and mechanical parts, so that the vehicle looked like a pile of scrap. Unfortunately, the unforeseen accident resulted in the loss of human lives: eleven were killed and many others injured.'

The experts maintained that the tyres were not suited to the function assigned to them. Further on, the judgement said: 'Such a conclusion from the experts undoubtedly perplexed the inquirers, indeed, the first consideration to emerge concerned the knowledge of the experts called upon to enlighten the Court. Though no one could object to Professor Speluzzi, a university don, well-founded doubts arose concerning the particular scientific and technical abilities of the engineer, Mr Mandella, a non-specialized graduate mostly concerned with construction, and the geometrician Rinaldi. No lay person could escape the conclusion that an experts' opinion of the sort required could not be entrusted to a geometrician.' A new board of experts was convened, and acquittal followed: Ferrari could finally relax. You cannot trifle with the law and his sigh of relief can easily be understood.

In November 1961 a 'bombshell' hit Modena. Eight of Ferrari's top managers left him. These were Chiti, Bizzarrini, and Galassi, all engineers, Selmi, the head of personnel, Gardini, the sales manager, Della Casa, the managing director, Giberti who was in charge of purchases, and Tavoni, the secretary and racing manager. The news was stunning. I remember a cartoon in the *Guerin Sportivo* showing eight men in a boat with the caption 'Eight men without a cox'. The reasons for this departure were unclear. Perhaps the eight managers wanted to control what was going on in the factory. Ferrari was taken unawares by this mass exodus in the same period as the death of Von Trips and fifteen spectators at Monza: an event which was still weighing heavily on his mind and on the motor-racing world in general.

But the real reason for the departure may be that Ferrari's wife was in the habit of wandering around the factory, interfering in everything. It seems that on some occasions she abused one or other of the managers for the pettiest of reasons. A couple of them therefore decided to leave and the others followed by way of solidarity. I talked to some of them later and they did not deny this to me. I have even heard that Laura once slapped Gardini.

In an illustrated weekly, I wrote: 'By leaving him, the eight have given back ten years of his life. The more he rages, the younger he gets. Enzo Ferrari from Maranello has returned to the environment that best suits him – that of the cold, purposeful, sometimes spiteful struggle. So they've left him – he'll just carry on alone. His friends, who are fewer than the fingers of one hand, as he likes to say, are, as usual, standing by him.'

He rolled up his sleeves. Inwardly he was shouting threats and punishments, but he managed to hide his feelings from the outside world. Then a couple of the fugitives returned and the others would later lend a hand in organizing the ATS, which was concerned with Formula 1 races and GT cars.

Ferrari said that he needed five years to make a new car and if these people were better than he was they would take two and a half years, but no one can perform miracles.

Everything gradually calmed down again, but Ferrari did not specify his programme for 1962. He did not hold the usual press conference until February, when he announced a period of intense activity. For many months, some thought that Ferrari had decided to give up. Since he was without a designer either for his racing cars or for the GT cars to sell to the wealthy all over the world, I mentioned the name of a young and capable technician to him – the person concerned was working for Maserati – Ferrari looked at me and said: 'No, he looks like a priest.'

There was intense activity, but Indianapolis was dropped, even though one car was already in an advanced stage of construction and another one was to follow soon after it. This was when the trustworthy Gianni Brera wrote: 'He has won all the races in the world except one – Indianapolis – which he will also win, because he has decided to do so and when Ferrari is fired by an idea, this idea sooner or later comes into being.'

Some years later Giovanni Agnelli told me that the programme for the Indy had to be postponed and that, perhaps, a Ferrari would never be seen at Indianapolis again . . .

In the summer of 1964, Ferrari asked for type-approval for a new car, the Le Mans berlinetta. He was not granted it and he therefore declared that he would not go to Monza for the Italian Grand Prix. However, he later changed his mind, perhaps because starting money for his single-seaters had been increased. Ferrari's strategy was simple: an Italian Grand Prix without Ferrari would be a minor race and if they wanted him, they would have to pay. The argument was flawless and Monza often had to meet the cost incurred by it. In the last weeks of 1976, war broke out between the Formula 1 manufacturers and the organizers of Grand Prix races. It was an intense struggle and all means were employed to win. One of the arguments was about dangerous circuits, the ones the manufacturers might reject.

Evangelisti interviewed Ferrari on behalf of the *Gazzetta dello Sport* and asked him whether the Formula 1 Constructors' Association (FOCA) would still race on 'certain courses such as the Monte Carlo and the tree-lined track at Monza'. Ferrari replied: 'Just a moment. It is true that some circuits present problems and Monte Carlo is a good example, but let's talk about Monza. My association with Monza started in 1923 and since then I have always had genuinely friendly relations with the organizers of that track, which has been the setting for many of my memories as both a racing-driver and a car manufacturer. I made my most recent demonstration of this attachment in 1976, when the car manufacturers and drivers had decided not to race at Monza. I had a meeting with the directors at Monza and I induced them to create two chicanes, which enabled me to obtain a change of mind on the part of my fellow car manufacturers.' Evangelisti then asked him about Imola and Ferrari replied: 'It is well-known that I am emotionally indebted to my friends in Imola, who have named their magnificent motor-racing track in memory of my son Dino and it is obvious that at my age I will see to the prompt settlement of this debt, so that it will not be left to my heirs.'

This, of course, meant that the 1977 Italian Grand Prix could be held at Imola. It appeared that in order to settle this emotional debt, Ferrari was prepared to turn his back on the Monza track and its directors who had treated him so generously in the past. However, it should also be remembered that Monza was certainly not ideal for Formula 1 races, so Ferrari's comment was not a complete betrayal.

In 1966 Ferrari did miss a Grand Prix. It was claimed that Italian general strikes affected even the Ferrari racing department and Ferraris did not go to the British Grand Prix. Ferrari gave the impression that there would be other absences but that is not how it turned out.

After three years, the threat to abandon Monza was repeated, but at the last moment was withdrawn. There would be other threats like this. The last, which turned out to be not just a threat, was the actual abandonment of racing after the 1976 German Grand Prix, in which Niki Lauda – the world championship title holder, who was on his way to his second consecutive success – so nearly lost his life.

15

Niki Lauda's arrival brings hope to Maranello

W hen the press release from Maranello appeared in the papers after the Nürburgring crash, I began to place bets on the date the Ferrari single-seaters would return to motor racing. The release, which was issued on the 5th August 1976, said: 'The Ferrari company would like to inform its friends in the racing world that having noted the interpretations of the rules made by the organizers of the Grand Prix races around the world, from Brazil onwards and culminating at the dramatic Nürburgring; in view of the lack of response from the FIA [the International motor-racing federation] to the judgements of the Automobile Club of Spain and of the international sports commission; offended that the same FIA did not even reply to the petition sent by Ferrari which pointed out that the procedure followed by court of appeal meant that our company would not be admitted; embittered by the lack of real legal and technical assistance from the Italian sports authorities; wishing to defend the honour of its sporting managers – the engineers Forghieri, Rocchi and Bussi, who have been rashly accused of technical incompetence; in order to allow the managing director of the company, Sguazzini, also to apply to the judiciary, having ascertained that sporting authorities, with their judgements, may also be defending interests that have nothing to do with their institutional purpose; the company has decided to suspend its participation in the world championship, with immediate effect.'

This announcement caused a stir and Ferrari settled down to wait. For years, his relations with the Italian sporting authorities had been somewhat stormy (and he was often right, because they did not defend him as they should have done); now Lauda was in a seriously ill condition and if he died, wild accusations would immediately ensue. The withdrawal allowed Ferrari a breathing space.

The next day, the papers were saying that Ferrari would probably return to racing at Monza. First there were the Austrian and Dutch Grand Prix races, but none of the single-seaters from Modena was present at the first event. I marked down the Dutch Grand Prix in my diary – I thought the Ferraris would reappear on that day. I was not wrong – but not through any merit on my part – my judgement was based on my experience of the Grand Old Man's way of thinking.

No one was better practised in the art of the comeback. 'I am leaving and you will see me no more,' he would say and then, when he was least expected, he would reappear on the tracks with his red racing-cars. At such a time a large part of what was written would concern Ferrari and his men. Some maintained that when Ferrari was making a come-back, he could ask for a higher fee, a special reward from the organizers.

On the 24th August, the headline of the *Corriere della Sera* read: 'Ferrari changes his mind and returns to racing' and 'Lauda back at the wheel in Canada within 40 days.'

But the world champion, no doubt urged on by his extraordinary physical strength, by his willpower and by Ferrari's action in looking for new drivers, caught everyone unawares and appeared in the Italian Grand Prix at Monza. When Niki turned up at Maranello in the days before the race, Ferrari observed him keenly. Later he said to a colleague of mine with *Il Giornale*: 'Nuvolari lost two sons. His indomitable, almost incredible, courage was perhaps even strengthened by these calamities. When he raced, he was looking for death, though he never found it in a car. Lauda managed to achieve by reason what Nuvolari had done instinctively. Lauda's ability to reason and his moral strength both helped him out of the abyss. The courage with which he has decided to return to racing was both the point of departure and the consequence of his rationality. When we knew he was in hospital in that condition, when we were waiting helplessly for hour after hour we had no idea of what could happen, of how he could have emerged from that terrible event at the Nürburgring. Now that we have seen him, he has gladdened our hearts.'

This was the driver that Ferrari wanted. Even though Lauda

returned to racing to make a point, to show Ferrari that he was not finished and that, before looking for other drivers, Ferrari should consider him, the car-maker was won over by this young man and his courage. It was not important that there could be a hidden dispute between him and his driver; what mattered was that Lauda reminded him of Nuvolari and that he was returning to racing because that was the only way to win back the world title. The Ferrari Formula 1 cars were no longer what they were at the beginning of the year – mostly because their rivals had improved – but with a little luck, in the sense of nothing happening to him, Lauda could regain his supremacy.

The struggle between him and the Englishman James Hunt was electrifying and it was not until the Japanese Grand Prix, the last of the year, that the winner of the 1976 world championship would be decided.

The decisive Japanese race was held on the 24th October and was won by Mario Andretti. James Hunt's third position won him the world title by just one point. Niki Lauda's withdrawal in the second lap inevitably provoked much discussion. People were amazed that a man like him, when faced with a choice between carrying on in very bad weather conditions and giving up the struggle for the world title, had gone for the second option. But I consider that, in Japan, Lauda had shown the measure of his proper view of sport, of still knowing how to choose between life and death. If the rain – which was dangerous both for the stability of the single-seater and because of the lack of visibility – had caused his car to end up diagonally across the middle of the track, this could have also been dangerous for the others. It is true that when Brambilla struggled with Hunt, overtook him rashly, was overtaken himself and started spinning like a top, it was, in a way, exciting, but it was the sort of behaviour that made you stop and think. Ferrari always told me that Vittorio Brambilla reminded him of Ascari senior, because of all the demands he made on his car and his determination to beat everyone else.

So Lauda retired and can he be blamed? It would be interesting to know what happened afterwards at Maranello. What would Ferrari have said and how would he react to his great driver's decision? I gave my opinion at the time and won't change it now: I thought the relationship between Ferrari and Lauda would change. Not that Ferrari could publicly attack his standard-bearer, but he must have felt something in his heart of hearts. Apart from anything else, he must have taken into account the fact that a driver is obliged to race whatever the circumstances and should not stop because the rain prevents him from seeing.

The fact remained that Lauda had stopped. It might be that in future the rain (it should not be forgotten that the Nürburgring accident was probably caused because the Ferrari skidded on a wet surface) would no longer intimidate the Austrian champion as it had in Japan. But Ferrari had to make a decision – and so did Lauda.

It was therefore probable that Lauda would leave, to be substituted by Emerson Fittipaldi, who had always dreamed of racing for Ferrari, even though he got a surprise when he first went to Maranello on a pilgrimage. He had expected Ferrari to talk to him about races, drivers and total commitment, but found himself answering questions about Brazilian women and whether they were beautiful and passionate. Fittipaldi did not realize that Ferrari behaved in this way so as not to let the driver think that he could be the Cavallino's saviour. By not attaching too much importance to racing, the car manufacturer was playing down his need for a driver such as Fittipaldi.

But even if Niki were to stay, I knew something would change. Ferrari's view of him would always be coloured by the memory of the Japanese race and this would not be favourable to relationship between the person preparing the car and the one who was supposed to drive it to victory. And what if Lauda were to stop racing? I did not think he would.

The following episode may shed some light on Niki Lauda the man. When he became world champion in the Italian Grand Prix at Monza, he had great trouble reaching his hotel. He had to spend hours satisfying the journalists. He waited with Regazzoni and Montezemolo to answer my questions which were live for the eight o'clock news. He was smiling more than usual. Finally he was at S. Eustorgio (the hotel at Arcore near Monza). It was then that Marielle asked him to go to Milan so they could celebrate the world title together. Niki looked at her and said: 'No, Marielle, it's not possible. This evening there's a dinner with all the men from the team. We can't leave. Try to understand.' When they arrived in the reception room they were both smiling. I was present and I approached to tell them both how pleased I was. They seemed serene and happy and yet an atmosphere of incomprehension had already grown between them and would later lead to their separation. That made me very sad. Perhaps Marielle had not been understood, either by Niki or by those around him. I would very much have liked to have known her better.

So Lauda was a man and not a computer, as many have maintained. A man with a heart and feelings, including the feeling of fear. Fear of fire, which is the most terrible enemy facing anyone who races cars. In this regard, it would be interesting to consider what happened to Nuvolari back in the spring of 1938, on the circuit at Pau.

His car suddenly burst into flames and he threw himself out of the cockpit. He had several burns and bruises and was taken to hospital. As the journalist and biographer of Nuvolari, Cesare De Agostini, mentions in his *L'Antileggenda di Nuvolari*, the champion decided to retire after this accident. When he was still in hospital, he sent two telegrams – one to the commissioner of the Automobile Club of Italy and the other to Gobbato, general manager of Alfa Romeo – in which he said that, having been greatly shocked by the serious accident, he was giving up racing. The telegram to Alfa was sent on the 16th April. The company replied on the 6th May and the letter was signed by an advisor and an attorney. The letter said: 'We have taken note of your intention – communicated to us in the telegram of the 16th April – to withdraw from racing competitions. Please accept our kind regards.'

For courageous men, for men who risk their lives, there is never any real understanding. As it was for Nuvolari in 1938, so it would be for Lauda in 1976. What they have achieved belongs to the past.

In early January 1977, a few hours before the Argentinian Grand Prix, news arrived in Buenos Aires that Lauda from Ferrari and Scheckter from Wolf were to exchange places. Would this be the start of a new chapter in the story of the relations between the man from Maranello and the misunderstood Lauda? Perhaps it would . . .

A few days after the Japanese Grand Prix, Ferrari held a press conference at Modena. When he mentioned Lauda and his fear because of the conditions in which he would have to race on the Japanese circuit, he admitted that he too had been too afraid to take part in the 1924 French Grand Prix, because he had had a nervous breakdown. It had taken 50 years for the truth about the 'flight from Lyon' to come out . . . better late than never.

There is no doubt that, after Dino, the men who counted most in Ferrari's life were his drivers. These were the men who, with their courage, their generosity, their fears and their faults, were largely responsible for the success of the red cars of Maranello. Ferrari always said there were drivers (but are there still?) who intentionally looked for death when they were racing.

De Portago used to say that racing-drivers are happier than other men because the closeness of death makes them experience life more fully. The noble Spaniard had a premonition of something. Before setting off in his last race, he gave Tavoni a note with the addresses of his mother and his wife, from whom he had been separated for some time. He had never done this before.

He was cremated and his wife had to scatter some of his ashes along the bobsleigh course at Saint-Moritz, where he had had 'many happy times'.

16

In search of the Red Devil

T his chapter reproduces my article from the magazine *Velocita* in 1963.

I was a small boy when Varzi and Nuvolari used to share between them their victories, their prizes and the affection of the Italians. I supported Achille and with him Juventus and Alfredo Binda. It could not have been otherwise – anyone who showed a preference for the black and white Turin club and the cyclist from Cittiglio almost always supported Varzi too. We were on the right side, on the side of class and style. The others were on the side of strength – they supported Ambrosiana Inter, Guerra and Nuvolari. Such a division was made without much subtlety and, it must be said, without much objectivity.

Varzi and Nuvolari. How could the sublime Varzi take lessons from someone who drove badly and looked as if he would go off the road at any moment? Achille was the very essence of coolness and composure, and seemed to be alien to the battles of the sports world, as did Juventus and Binda. Tazio Nuvolari and Achille Varzi were the cause of many arguments and many insults. I often saw them race. This was the very least that could be done in the case of Mille Miglia, since it went straight through our district. We, however, often went further on up on the Cisa [a mountain pass] or to the bends before Cremona to see (or rather to catch a glimpse of) our heroes. The circuit revealed the differences between the two champions. At Cremona, at Alessandria in the race dedicated to Bordino, when Nuvolari flew off the road because Comotti would not let him pass, at the race at Monza, when Von Stuck's Auto Union won and Nuvolari managed to insert himself between two cars which had spun and were blocking his path, I had to recognize that Tazio did things other drivers would never dream of doing. But my heart and my instincts were for Varzi.

Years passed and I had the good fortune to enter the automobile world. I got to know Canestrini, Ferrari, Jano, Amorotti, Ugolini, many drivers – in other words, all the men who, in one way or the other, had contributed to the creation of the formidable duo. From the accounts of technicians, journalists and enthusiasts, I discovered another side to Varzi and Nuvolari, which was different to that known by the man in the street. Maturity had meanwhile made me more objective in my judgements. I began to recognize that Nuvolari was different from the others and when I had the opportunity to talk to him, I realized that behind this tired man was a story of much pain and suffering. I started to respect him and I rightly forgot about the 'rages' he had inflicted on me by beating *my* Achille.

Now, many years after his death, I have finally got to know the real Tazio Nuvolari. Giulio Cesare Castello, one of Italy's most shrewd film critics, is in his early forties. A studious man of letters and a teacher at the *Centro Sperimentale di Cinematografia* [experimental cinematography centre], he has always had a fascination about Nuvolari. He knows everything about the 'Flying Mantuan' – he even remembers the titles of papers containing the most flattering comments – he knows all the photographs and dates. He too, should have met Nuvolari. Castello has a different temperament from mine and is averse to passion. Some time ago, he was asked to make a television programme on whatever subject he liked. Castello did not hesitate – he would do a portrait of Nuvolari. He telephoned me and I was very happy to accompany him on his voyage of discovery about the champion.

For many days, we had only one topic of conversation – Nuvolari and motor-racing. We left Milan and headed for Gardone Riviera, where Tazio's wife Carolina lives. She was not there, having gone to Mantova (Mantua) for a few days. We contacted her by telephone and she was happy to see us there. When we arrived, we saw that a delivery-boy had got there a few seconds before us – Carolina wanted to greet her guests with a house full of flowers.

We said hello and met the family lawyer, who wanted to satisfy himself that there would be nothing damaging in the interview. Then the lady, who had suffered the loss of an irreplaceable man, started a long soliloquy.

We went into Tazio's study, where we were not allowed to touch anything, just to look reverently. Carolina's voice, which was sometimes quiet, sometimes excited, took us into a world that seems unreal today. Tazio was there with us, brought to life by the words of his wife, with dozens of photographs and accounts of episodes previously unknown to us. The telegram from D'Annunzio who made him swear to win the Targa Florio (which of course he did, how could it have been otherwise?), the first photograph of Tazio at the wheel of a racing car, his racing clothes, his trophies, the list of motorcycles and cars he raced in. Carolina's voice had been relaxed, but became more animated as she started talking about the real Tazio, about what he did in this car or that, paying no attention to personal sacrifices or danger. 'We were in Verona for the Circuito del Pozzo and Tazio was getting dressed for the race. Dressing was like a ceremony for him, just as it is for a bullfighter. He always took a long time over it. Suddenly he said to me: "Carolina, isn't it sad that I'm going to beat the great Bordino? He's a famous champion and I'm just a novice. And yet I must beat him. It's my duty." That was what Nuvolari was like – a daredevil, but worrying about beating a famous driver.

There followed hundreds of other memories, from intimate ones, such as when they saw each other for the first time and told each other with their eyes that they would always live together, to memories of their sons, who both died at 18 years of age, with 9 years between them, to Nuvolari's illness and his visit to Padre Pio. 'When he got back he didn't say a word. I knew never to disturb him from his thoughts. After hours of obstinate silence, he said to me: "It's just as good this way." He already knew about death. Racing had consumed him. He died, destroyed by his passion, by his burning desire to race and always to win.'

As far as Carolina Nuvolari was concerned, no other racing-drivers, or anyone else, existed in her memory. There was just Tazio.

After a telephone call, we went to see Decimo Compagnoni, Nuvolari's faithful mechanic. His was a peaceful home, with a very nice wife and children. He was another great source of memories – about the Nuvolari who became an engineer, who required mechanical improvements from Compagnoni that implied a deep knowledge of the secrets of a car. So it was not true that Tazio used to break everything? No, it was not true. Giulio Cesare Castello was in a trance. His Nuvolari was without rival. There were more memories of battles at 200kph, behind-the-scenes accounts of races and men.

We left Mantova at nine in the evening. The fog and the ice were exasperating for our driver. We got lost several times and had to get out to look at the street signs. Ironically, whilst we were making such slow progress, we still had memories of the mad speeds of Nuvolari to keep us company. We arrived in Modena after three unforgettable hours. The next morning Ferrari was expecting us.

Ferrari found it hard to talk about the past, perhaps because Varzi and Nuvolari were the only drivers who always looked him in the eye. But he eventually started to unwind and tell us about his memories. It became clear that his preference was for Tazio. Varzi was a different type, he had a different style and was too much of a gentleman for a red-blooded man like Ferrari. 'What do you want me to tell you about a champion – who was already a legend in his own lifetime?' His comments went on in the same vein, without a clear outline, but held together by subtle eloquence. Then he became more thoughtful and we started to hear some interesting things. Some of our crew were moved to tears . . . Ferrari had hit the bull's eye once again.

Nello Ugolini arrived and told us of the time at the Nürburgring in 1935, when Tazio, who was waiting at the start with a great line-up of Auto Unions and Mercedes, wanted Ugolini to get a new Italian flag to put on the flagpole after the race. The tricolour belonging to the organizers was torn and faded. 'I asked him why he had made this request and he replied that it was because he was going to win. I looked at him in amazement. He flew off into the fog, in an Alfa half the size of the arrogant German cars, he did incredible and immensely intelligent things and he won. As soon as he returned to the pit, he asked me if I had found the new, intact flag. The crowd, which after a long moment of astonishment, was cheering him, did not interest him. He wanted a brightly-coloured flag without repair patches to be flying up there over German soil. He looked up into the sky with a radiant face. That is what Tazio Nuvolari was like.'

From Modena, we went to Milan to see Canestrini. The 'patriarch' of motor-racing journalism was on the opposite side to Ferrari. He was for Varzi and never tired of repeating it. But he acknowledged exceptional qualities in Nuvolari – unrivalled courage and resolve.

He replied to what Castello and I told him about our previous interviews with his own version, which was cool and scrupulous, devoid of all passion. He said that Nuvolari was a wise administrator, that he had come to a perfect financial arrangement with Varzi, that they knew they had to put on a first-rate show for the public, which was something they always managed to do. This was another aspect of Nuvolari – a wise administrator, who knew very well what fruits fame could provide for him and for Varzi. The image of the wild racer Nuvolari was fading away. The great Tazio was a man who had everyday problems, and was capable of considered action just like a common mortal.

After Canestrini, we spoke to Nino Farina, the first world champion after the war. 'Many consider that I was Tazio's pupil and it's true. I was a pupil who managed to beat all the champions, even the most famous, but I never beat Nuvolari. And it's right that it should have been so. I did not deserve to. What I saw him do will never be seen again. Thirty years ago he was driving with the techniques of today. When Stirling Moss told me some time ago that he had learnt the straight-arm style of driving from me, I told him that I, in turn, had learnt from the great Tazio. Everyone has learnt from him, even if some may not wish to acknowledge it. There will never be another Nuvolari.'

Then we went to Portello to see Giovanbattista Guidotti, the man who was by Nuvolari's side in many races, including three Mille Miglias: one of which went down in history because of the headlight affair. There are many different versions of this story: how could it be otherwise? We asked Guidotti about the headlights. 'Yes, it's true. But it only happened for a moment. Tazio turned out the headlights only when we were right behind Achille, to make him think that we had stopped. After a long and frantic chase, we had managed to catch up with him. Varzi knew that it was us on his heels and we knew that it was him in front. He was going so fast that it could only be Achille. When we were a few hundred yards behind, Tazio turned out the headlights for a moment. When he turned them on again, we were in front of Varzi. That's all'

Next stop Turin, and the *Museo dell' Automobile*, where we were to meet Vittorio Jano, the creator of the famous Alfa Romeo of that time. Dear Jano, so straight-forward and human. For him, Tazio is still 'The Lad'. He told us of when Antonio Ascari, who, like Nuvolari, was from Castel d'Ario, started recommending Tazio to him. 'Until one day, at Monza, I put him behind the wheel of a P2. After half a lap, he flew off the track but miraculously stayed alive. I didn't want to see him again. Years passed. Then one evening I found him at home begging my wife to let him try again. He was a sensible driver who had an exceptional feeling for mechanical things. He drove faster than the others and came back with his engine all in order and with his brakes almost intact, unlike others – even some of the great ones – who used up the brake linings as if they were butter.'

Vittorio Jano was also for Tazio. The satisfaction Tazio had given him and the sensational victories he had won were only the visible fruits of an unequalled career. 'He was a man in the truest sense of the word. He never wanted to be given one car rather than another – he always preferred the others to choose before him and took whatever was left. And he still won. He had respect for himself and for his opponents. He was full of spirit. With a driver like him, we never went home beaten.'

In this rapid account of a moving pilgrimage, I have omitted the question we asked everyone. Was it true that Tazio Nuvolari wanted to die at the wheel of a racing car? The answers were quite varied and I will respect what was perhaps the most dramatic episode in Nuvolari's life by remaining silent.

Tazio lived intensely, as few others have.

'He died, destroyed by his passion' – Carolina Nuvolari told us – 'and for me it was as if he had been killed at the wheel of a red Alfa Romeo just after winning a race.'

When Alfa Romeo inaugurated its magnificent *Museo Storico* at Arese on December 18th, 1976, Carolina Nuvolari was also present. Looking very elegant and in great form, despite her years, she looked at the cars which her Tazio had driven to victory. I asked her what in her opinion had been the secret of her partner's greatness. Her reply was decisive: 'His immense attachment to his work and his great courage.' After a pause, she went on: 'And perhaps I helped too, because I never bothered him with jealousies, exhortations, pleas to come home quickly and all the things a wife usually says to her husband.' She was proud of this statement and she added: 'And since there are not many years left for me, when I go, I ask you journalists to write only that Carolina Nuvolari, faithful wife of Tazio, whom she has never betrayed even in thought since she was 17, is dead.'

17

At last - the agreement with Fiat

A little while after the pilgrimage described in the previous Chapter, Ferrari launched the *Premio Giornalistico Dino Ferrari* [the Dino Ferrari Prize for Journalism] in memory of his son. At that time my relations with Ferrari were not good. There had been difficult situations and misunderstandings and he had accused me of wanting to impose on him certain decisions that were his concern only. The factory and racing had nothing to do with these decisions – they were personal matters.

In May I confided in a friend in Modena, who was an employee of Ferrari's and I revealed knowledge of certain attitudes and situations to him.

I went back to Milan and the next day I received two telegrams – one at the office and the other at home. The text in each was the same and it was from Ferrari, who was telling me to get in touch with him because he needed to speak to me urgently. I telephoned Gozzi, the press secretary of the factory and one of Ferrari's trusted men. He told me to wait for Lorenzo Bandini at eight o'clock in front of the RAI building in Corso Sempione in Milan.

I stayed in the office without having any dinner. I spoke to a friend who asked me what could possibly be so urgent. I calmly replied: 'He wants to sue me, that's all. Or rather, he wants to frighten me.'

When Lorenzo arrived in a powerful 5-litre Ferrari Super America, he was the one who was frightened. He immediately asked me what I had done to Ferrari, who was in a bad temper and told me I was mad to enrage him. Good old Lorenzo – he was so worried about it. The trip we took from the Corso Sempione to Modena was very quick, but long enough for Lorenzo to reproach me and to beseech me to stay calm.

We arrived at the Ristorante Fontana, in Piazza Garibaldi, in the building that belonged to Ferrari. Today the restaurant is called Tucano. It had been something of a disappointment for Ferrari, who thought it would become a popular meeting place. The food and drink are good, but I know that it is not all that Ferrari had hoped for.

Gozzi was waiting for me and the frightened Bandini disappeared. Gozzi greeted me, then went off to call Ferrari. The latter arrived and asked me if I had eaten and, as soon as I said no, he sat me at a table.

He immediately asked me if I knew why he had wanted me to come and see him. I replied that I did and that it was because he wanted to sue me. He was surprised. Then he repeated to me the distorted version that his employee-friend had given him. I replied point by point, denying what was not true and acknowledging what was. I was not frightened of Ferrari. I knew that he respected me too much to hit me. I said to him: 'Ferrari, if you sue me, I will stop working and live quietly for the rest of my life.' He didn't understand what I meant and, underneath, I didn't really understand either! It was just something to say.

'You said that I am a tax evader. You said that I have 900 million lire in ready assets in a bank in Modena. You said that I earn one million lire net on each car I sell.' I replied that I had not said it, but one of his employees had. I had just repeated it to his 'employee-friend'.

The minutes passed and he grew calmer, though in fact he had never lost control. On the other hand, in January, when he and I had been eating with Giulio Cesare Castello and Gozzi, there had been a terrible scene. He had shouted, with unrepeatable curses, for someone to bring him a pill so that he could continue to breathe. Gozzi was fanning him. Castello went pale and would always remember the encounter.

We were coming to the end of our meeting and Ferrari had understood that perhaps I was not as guilty as he had thought. He did not tell me so, but I thought that this was the case. He wanted to know whether it was true that, as he had been told, I intended to write a book about him. I said it was not true and that it would be too easy to get rich.

Finally he told me that an important Italian weekly needed a journalist for its motor-racing column. If I was interested, I could send him my *curriculum vitae* and he would forward it to the editor of the publication along with his recommendation.

At nearly three in the morning, Gozzi took me to the station. Just to be witty, I asked where Bandini was and he told me that racing-drivers had to go to bed early.

I sent off my *curriculum vitae,* but I had no illusions about getting the job. A few days later, Evangelisti asked me if he could send off my piece on Nuvolari for the Dino Ferrari prize. In the old days, you had to queue up, but now it was up to the judges to decide. I said no.

A few days later, Ferrari telephoned me to ask me if I could put in writing what I had told him about the bank account, etc. I wrote back to him immediately, including the name of the person who had made the inferences, and below my signature I added: 'There's no harm in also being your executor.' I knew this would annoy him, but I was not sorry. By now, arguments had become quite frequent between us.

In August 1962, I had asked him for an appointment and he asked me to go to Maranello early. At eight o'clock, I found him in Modena, at the barbers. When he came out to go to the cemetery, he said he would see me a little later in the factory.

I was there, but he didn't see me until 7.45 in the evening. He had been busy. We went to the restaurant and spoke about various trivial matters – he was wasting time. Then he asked me what it was that I wanted. With a slightly trembling voice, I asked him for a loan of three quarters of a million lire. I needed the money for a friend who was in difficulties. He looked at me impassively. Then he said: 'Alright, come to Modena on Monday and I will go with you to the bank to endorse the withdrawal. Then you can make arrangements with your own bank.' I never came. Later he would say that the only person in the world who did not want to be paid for a job was Rancati. This sort of attitude surprised him and the fact that someone could send him back 100,000 lire for work done on Ferrari's behalf astonished him.

A few months later, Evangelisti told me that Canestrini, chairman of the panel of judges for the prize, had told him: 'We are down to a short-list of two – Camilla Cederna, for an article in *Espresso* and Gino. But Camilla has only been interested in cars once in her life. Gino is one of us, and his piece on Nuvolari is really well done.' I rebuked Evangelisti for entering my article but, with his usual good sense, he pointed out that the 500,000 lire prize was not to be sneezed at.

In October, a series of articles I had written entitled *Gli anni nero dell' Invincible* ['The dark years of the invincible one'] appeared in *Il Giorno*. They formed a rather critical, even mischievous, study of the bad moves made by Ferrari and of what he had copied from his competitors. He wrote to me: 'Dear Rancati, I have just read "the dark years of the invincible one" in Monday's copy of *Il Giorno*. In your eyes I was, and still am, someone who was carried along – as I am in the eyes of people who, because they were born too late, do not know that dark years come to everyone. However, thank you for the thought and best wishes. Ferrari.'

Meanwhile, the date of the press conference and of the nomination of the prize winner was approaching. Evangelisti assured me that I was the winner and we joked together, saying that it was nevertheless too early to start spending the money.

The morning of the meeting came and, before the press conference, Canestrini stood up to read out the results. Athos looked at me and I at him and when the winner's name was announced, we discovered that the prize was going to a colleague. I shall never forget Evangelisti's face. I took the result well and recognized that, after all, I had not deserved to win.

Relations with Ferrari started to improve slowly and at the 1964 press conference he wrote a dedication in his book, *Le mie gioie terribili* [My terrible joys] to me, with the words: 'To Gino Rancati, who is no longer an orphan.' He was still the same, in speech and in writing. Oddone Camerana, Fiat's publicity manager, said that Ferrari wrote very well. He added: 'Ferrari writes with an extraordinarily personal style, sometimes reminiscent of that of C.E. Gadda, in some of its lively construction which suggests indignation, dissatisfaction and aggressiveness.

Let us return once more to 1963, a very important year in the Ferrari story. It was at this time that the repercussions of the Ford affair in Bologna were felt.

When Ferrari bought and later resold the building which belonged to Ford of Italy, a long dialogue started between him and the men from the great American company. In May, a Ford manager telephoned him and two days later, came to meet Ferrari in Modena.

It is easy to see why Ford was interested in acquiring the small and prestigious Emilian company and their interest set various trains of events in motion which would later, in my opinion, wash away the shame of 1918, when Ferrari failed to be taken on by Fiat. Although he had obtained great satisfaction by beating the cars from Turin with Alfa cars, the account was not yet fully paid.

Ferrari had for some time been thinking about the future of his company. Dino was dead and there was no heir to continue the progress of either the industry or the racing. What could he do? He had to find an answer – an Italian answer. It should not be forgotten that Ferrari was a convinced nationalist and it would not have surprised me if he had left instructions for his body to be buried in the Italian flag. Above Dino's portrait in Ferrari's office at Maranello were three plastic roses – one white, one red and one green. So he might sell the Ferrari company, but only to Italians. If Fiat were later to enter the negotiations, so much the better.

Having been rejected as an engineer and test-driver, he would finally join the big FIAT family as an associate. Ferrari also knew that Giovanni Agnelli liked his company. He had always had a particular feeling for racing cars and the Ferrari company was, after all, the best in the world.

Negotiations continued, with the Americans showing determined interest coupled to intricate and detailed negotiation. Then Ferrari discovered that they were in effect tying his hands with small print: perhaps he should not have been surprised? He was pathetic when he said that having voiced his fears the reply he was given humiliated him: "But Mr. Ferrari, you are selling your company and yet you want to be able to carry on managing it as you like?" Ferrari replied although this was not true of the industrial sector, it was true of the experimental racing side, where the very complex bureaucratic laws were obviously not in harmony with the spirit required. Then he asked the member of the American negotiating team who seemed to me to be the most interested: 'Up to what limit can you take an agreement without preliminary authorization from Detroit?' He replied: 'Up to ten thousand dollars.' Ferrari said his anger changed into depression.' Now, is it not strange that a man sent by Ford to acquire Ferrari could only spend up to 10,000 dollars, or the cost of just one Ferrari car?

In my opinion, Ferrari wanted to make it known to certain people that he could hand over everything to a dangerous competitor – not just the racing side (for its publicity value) but also the industrial side . . . That is why, and this is still my opinion, the operation that was to lead to the Ferrari-Fiat agreement began to take shape in 1963. With that agreement, Ferrari would enjoy the feeling of having fully avenged himself. He was a man who did not forget, and who knew how to wait.

Meanwhile Ford, humiliated by their failure, decided to go back to racing – since they had not managed to acquire Ferrari's company, they would beat his cars instead. With all the strength of their organization, they prepared a sports racing car for the car constructor's world championship. They won the world title in 1966 and in 1968. They also made a V8 engine which, in Cosworth form, was to dominate Formula 1 racing for many years. In fact cars fitted with the Cosworth-Ford engine were often to beat Ferrari in the world championships. The Vanwell had taken its revenge on Ferrari and now it was Ford's turn. But Ferrari was still steaming ahead and this is where his strength lay: by continuing to race, he never wasted time in an activity where staying still even for a few months means having to make up lost ground bit by bit – a necessity which is sometimes not possible.

As Gianni Rogliatti mentions in his interesting and thorough book *Le Ferrari* ['Ferrari cars'], Pier Ugo Gobbato arrived at Maranello in May 1965. He was the son of the Gobbato who had been general manager of Alfa Romeo for years and who had had Enzo Ferrari as one of his closest collaborators. Gobbato junior, a man of undoubted skill, was to show both Ferrari and Lancia – where he later became general manager – that he was a worthy successor to his father. Gobbato knew what he wanted and was far-sighted, but he was not very easy to get on with, which sometimes led to misunderstandings and disagreements. Perhaps few understand him better than I, for I too am considered to be 'difficult'. The word makes me laugh. In Italy, when they want to get rid of someone because he knows his job, because he loves the truth and because he does not waver this way and that, they accuse him of being difficult and the result is guaranteed. No doubt about it.

When Gobbato arrived at Maranello, the first act of Ferrari's new vengeance had already started.

133

Ferrari wanted to make a Formula 2 single-seater but in order to do this he needed an homologated engine (one of which at least 500 units had been made), but this production target was beyond his production capabilities. On the 1st March 1965, it was announced that Fiat would adopt the Dino engine (which was suitable for Formula 2) for one of its next GT cars, to be called the Fiat Dino and which would be made in both a coupé and a spider version. The announcement started rumours in the car world and in April Fiat made it known that it was not true that they had acquired the Maranello factory and that the agreement about the Fiat-Dino would not go any further than the requirements of the Emilian manufacturer.

But the venture did not produce the desired results. The GT car, which was one of the most eagerly-awaited, met with a modest success and the Formula 2 car would last for one short season – a disappointing end to an agreement that could have been much more profitable for both Fiat and Ferrari. However, what mattered to Ferrari was that he had linked up with the Mirafiori firm.

Finally, on Saturday the 21st July 1969 at 4.30pm, the following announcement was made by Fiat: 'Following a meeting between the chairman of Fiat, Dr Giovanni Agnelli, and the engineer Mr Enzo Ferrari, it has been decided that, with the aim of ensuring continuity of development for the Ferrari company, the present arrangement of technical collaboration with Fiat will within the year be changed into one of joint participation.

A few days before the announcement, Ferrari had sworn that he was going to retire at the Italian Grand Prix on the 7th of September. What can we make of this?

I commented on the agreement in *Il Giorno*: 'Ferrari has now achieved the masterpiece of his lifetime. He has interested – let us put it that way – Fiat to the point that they have absorbed him. This is his greatest victory. Fifty years have passed since Ferrari was refused a job with Fiat. Today he is on the verge of returning, as an associate, to Mirafiori. It has been a long half century. The man from Maranello has spent it working hard and allowing himself no holidays or hobbies. Making use of his instinct for financial matters, he has built an empire worth several thousand million lire. Motor-racing has made him rich, while it has caused others to lose even the shirt on their back. This is another of his great achievements. Wouldn't we like this man to try to flourish again, even if it were only for one day? This is why he will never withdraw from racing. He will always continue to move forward, even if it means – as it has meant all his life – having to compete with his opponents in the workshop before he meets them on the racing track.'

A couple of days later, I received a letter from a friend of mine and of Ferrari's who reproached me for the article in *Il Giorno* and said: 'I do not understand the way you have tackled your theme and the way you express your point of view. I hope that I am wrong because, if not, I should be very sorry about the loss of whatever favourable opinion I may have formulated about you.'

The poor friend died before I could talk to him about it.

After the Fiat-Ferrari agreement, *Der Spiegel* said: 'Fiat has taken a 50 per cent share-holding in the Ferrari company to help the racing giant out of its financial difficulties.' I do not think that Ferrari had economic problems: he only wanted to ensure the continuity of his company. It was more likely that, if the agreement had not been made, we would have read in the papers that the Ferrari company was abandoning racing. This is not a wild hypothesis.

Some have reported that Ferrari got 2,150,000,000 lire for half of his company.

About this period, Ferrari wrote: '. . . I was thinking about all this, on that day, the 18th June 1969, when I went up to the eighth floor in the Corso Marconi, where the Fiat offices are. I was shown into Gianni Agnelli's office. I had known him 20 years before, but had met him only four times since. One day, he had come to Maranello to collect a prototype with central steering and coachwork by Pininfarina. He himself had wanted it to be made that way. Now I was seeing him in a different situation. It was the final act of a story that had been maturing for a long time. "Go ahead, Ferrari, I'm listening," he said to me, in his elegant and confident way.

'I spoke for a long time. He did not interrupt. I spoke about my past, my present and the future of the factory. I was able to expound my thoughts fully, as never before. Then Agnelli spoke. He was more than 20 years younger than me. I noted his strength – the strength of a modern man, of a politician and diplomat of the business world – and I noted his lively and agile mind. His questions were short and to the point – the questions of a man who wants to find out and wants to reach agreement. In the end, he called his colleagues in and concluded: "Well, Ferrari, is it true that this agreement could have been reached before?" He turned to his associates, "Gentleman, perhaps we have lost time: now we must make up for it."

'I left Turin late at night and, according to my habit, went back to Modena. I felt happy that I had found the right destination for my company and happy that I had secured continuity for my colleagues and workers. In Maranello, I gave my name to a company making cars that are famous throughout the world. Fiat had made a real car factory.'

I never asked him how he got to the eighth floor. He never used lifts but on that occasion he must have been obliged to use a means of transport which he did not like.

Some time later, he told me that the Ferrari company's capital was divided up as follows: 49 per cent to him, 40 per cent to Fiat, 10 per cent to his son Piero and 1 per cent to Pininfarina. He added: 'When I die, my 49 per cent will go to Fiat.'

But the subdivision he described was not accurate. Pininfarina never had a 1 per cent holding in the Ferrari company. Why should he mislead me? I have never been able to understand it.

18

All the Commendatore's men

In March 1971, I received the following letter, dated the 3rd: 'Dear Rancati, When I finally got back to the office, I found Dondo upset and annoyed. He has reason to be. He abandoned, on my suggestion, the press conference in order to reserve the 365/GT/4 launch for TV, however the TV report did not go out and the press conference can no longer be held. I realize his disappointment but I also realize the futility of maintaining relations with a company which I shall refrain from judging. My friend Gino will always be able to remember Ferrari, for reasons that personally concern him: in future please don't talk to me about TV, since I do not want to suffer again consequences like those of today.'

However, he would change his mind, after not a little persuasion. He had said to me several times that before he died he would like to talk live on the television for one hour. He confessed that this was 'one of the few satisfactions I have yet to enjoy.' On the instructions of my superiors, I many times proposed an hour-long programme to him, which would also contain clips of wins and important races from the past. He always replied: 'Just wait a little longer and then we'll do it.' This 'little longer' never came to an end, although at one point it seemed that he would finally have the satisfaction of his live programme. The programme *Ring* offered him the chance and he got his press secretary to ask me if it would be worthwhile. I gave him a favourable opinion, but I did not add that I would be sad not to be present myself on the day.

Then he had to cancel the programme. The reason for the cancellation was an old habit he had got into twenty years before: he would never sleep away from home. In those twenty years, I only once saw him go into an hotel room, during Ferrari practices at Monza. If he took part in the *Ring* programme, he would have to spend the night in Rome and this was unacceptable to him. They then thought of moving the studio to Modena. But the television journalists would finish working on the news just before it went on the air. They would have to leave Rome in the early afternoon. The problems were insoluble and so Enzo Ferrari never appeared on the programme. He said nothing to me about it, but I knew he must have been very sorry about it.

At the end of 1966, Ferrari telephoned me to say that he did not intend to organize his usual end-of-year press conference. However, he hinted that he would be quite happy to have it on television: just himself and a few journalists, who would have a round-table discussion. I immediately mentioned this to Aldo Assetta, the chief editor in Turin, and one of the few real personalities in television journalism. He was also a gentleman of the old school – in other words, he was a colleague and a rare friend. Thus the conference was organized. Obviously, the journalists invited to take part would have to be suitable for Ferrari and we did try to present him with a list that was agreeable. But he was responsible for turning people down, not us. The recorded programme went on the air and there were some who complained to him about not being invited. There was only one reply to this: 'Talk about it to the TV company, we just did what they told us to do.'

This was a strange attitude. But lies were compulsory at the Ferrari company, and not just because of the boss's inclination; perhaps they thought they would be pleasing him?

One summer's day Franco Gozzi, who was much more than just Ferrari's press secretary, was in his office. It was hot, the windows were open and the noise of two Formula 1 single-seaters could be heard: Ickx and Merzario were testing them on the company's test track at Fiorano. The telephone rang and Gozzi picked it up. 'Oh, hello, how are you? Yes, we'll have to go out for a meal around here when evening falls and it's cooler. Who? No, they're not here. Ickx is in Belgium and I don't know where Merzario is – perhaps he's abroad. I'm sorry I can't help you. Goodbye.' The other person present was astonished, but began to understand – he had only just arrived at Maranello – how the President's men behaved.

You 'phone Ferrari and ask for the Commendatore. The

switchboard, where only men work, tells you that he's not there. So you get yourself put through to someone else, say nothing about the first reply and you find that Ferrari is in after all. This strange behaviour was also adopted after 1969 by the important people in the Fiat-Ferrari alliance.

In view of the atmosphere there, it may be thought that not answering straight away was a way of gaining time in order to prepare for the conversation. Why is he ringing me up? What is this about? This could be the reasoning. Then, after a quick review of the situation, they are ready to reply. This is not a fanciful explanation.

At the beginning of 1976, Montezemolo and I decided to go to the Spanish Grand Prix. He said he would see Ghedini about reserving the rooms and everything else to do with the trip. Then Luca threw himself into Umberto Agnelli's election campaign. A few days before the race, I called Ghedini in Maranello. He was not there. He rang me back later and said: 'Gino, I've just come from the press office. Unfortunately, there are no more rooms, not even for Monte Carlo.' Obviously I was being made to pay for some offence I had committed. There is never any harm in checking, so I rang up the Hotel Barajas in Madrid and they told me I could have as many rooms as I wanted . . .

Also in March 1973, Ferrari wrote to me:' . . . but are you really fated to stay at all costs in the world of show business? You can write, you have passion and memories. Why weep over a choice? If only to consider that among so many roads, you have chosen the most thankless one.'

On April 19th, I received another message: 'I have not seen *Domenica Sportiva* nor did I know that Andretti was already in Italy, if I had known I would have advised him against it. Whilst I confirm my letter of the 3rd March, I would be interested to know who chartered the plane for Andretti and his wife so that they could arrive in time for the programme. I am waiting for my people to return!'

1971 was not a positive year for the Ferrari company. There was a rather worrying crisis. Fiat were not happy with how Ferrari's racing was proceeding. At the end of the season, on the 1st October, Giovanni Agnelli received two journalists – Lorenzo Pilogallo from the *Corriere della Sera* and myself. Also at the meeting were two managers from the factory. Pilogallo in his calm way and I with my enthusiasm described the situation the Ferrari company was in, and we also pointed out the necessity of using link men who knew how to deal with people at the Ferrari company.

Pilogallo said that it would be appropriate to send a reliable man to Maranello, in the same way that Boniperti was sent to Juventus. I added that a suitable candidate could be the young Cristiano Rattazzi, Susanna's son and therefore Agnelli's nephew. The chairman of Fiat replied that there were other plans for Cristiano. The meeting lasted for almost an hour – much longer than the twenty minutes originally arranged. Perhaps the idea of Luca Montezemolo at Ferrari was born on that day?

In the evening, a frightened Pilogallo rang me up. Ferrari had telephoned him to say that he had already been told about the meeting by the wife of a driver. I smiled – there had been no wife, all that had happened was that one of the two managers had immediately informed Ferrari.

One week later, at the Paris motor show, Agnelli was talking to Ferry Porsche when he saw me. He left Porsche and led me to a corner of the Fiat stand. He began: 'Rancati, it was unpleasant with Ferrari last week . . .' I interrupted: 'If you knew Ferrari, you wouldn't say that.' He replied: 'But I haven't got time to get to know a 73-year-old man.'

When I returned from Paris, I wrote the following letter to a friend: 'Yesterday, Pilogallo rang me at nine in the evening. He is still very worried because he has found out that manager X told Ferrari about our conversation with the Fiat chairman. He apparently reacted furiously. I am not worried, our information was not gratuitous but was the necessary and inevitable reply to a request for information. On the other hand, I am surprised because the manager did not so much breach our trust as that of his real employer. I would like you to know that as soon as we have confirmation of the leak, Pilogallo and I will ask you to arrange for us to meet the chairman. We consider we have the right and the duty to do this in order to continue the sincere impulse which encouraged us during the conversation of the 1st October and which encouraged me during the encounter in a Paris, which I told you about on the telephone.'

By now, contacts with Ferrari had become more and more rare. The ups and downs of our relationship kept us apart. But I did not forget him, nor did he forget me. In March 1974, I went to see him and I wrote an article about the meeting. Afterwards, I received a few lines dated the 22nd March: 'Dear Rancati, As it says in *Auto70*, Ferrari at 74 "drives as well and as decisively as ever". How is this possible with the legislation that is currently in force? Thank you and kind regards.'

Despite his years, he was still lively and quick-witted. The legislation forbad people under 21 and over 65 to drive vehicles that went faster than 180kph. Because of this, Ferrari drove a 1600cc Fiat 131 automatic.

When the company presented the Ferrari 400 Automatic at the 1976 Paris Exhibition, perhaps I could claim just a little of the credit. I had spoken about it so many times with the managing director of the factory (first Dondo, then Fusaro) and with Ferrari and they had finally satisfied me.

I was at Modena in April 1974 and I told Ferrari that I would like to go to the Spanish Grand Prix 'as a tourist'. I specified that I would pay my own costs, but when the trip was arranged, Sante Ghedini told me that I owed nothing because I would be going as a guest of the Ferrari company. The Spanish Grand Prix of that year marked the start of the trail that would bring Regazzoni near to winning the world title that year and allow Niki Lauda to win it the following year. I realized at once that Luca Montezemolo had equipped the team with qualities that it had lacked for some time: order, good manners, good relations with the press and, above all, a good understanding with the drivers.

I observed Lauda from the top of the tower which overlooks the entire Jarama circuit and which allows a race to be well understood, and I was convinced that he had great driving skills. He also knew just what he wanted in the pits, where it is not always easy to make yourself understood. The trials confirmed that the Ferraris were in good shape. All sorts of people gathered around the glorious Maranello company – and not just Italians. On the Saturday afternoon, I was going back to the hotel in a Fiat 127 driven by Clay Regazzoni. There was an underpass just before the exit to the circuit and in front of it were two policemen. Clay said to me: 'Shall we make them jump?' Before I understood what he meant, he accelerated towards them. When we were just a few metres away he did an expert about-face. Without a moment's pause, we were shooting towards Madrid. Who would do this sort of thing today? I am certain no one would. But Clay was a driver from a different era and the photographic report published in *Playboy* (the Italian edition of November 1976) confirmed how distant the Ticinese driver was from the deliberate and calculating world of motor-racing as it had become.

Let us return to the Jarama circuit. After the start, Peterson surged ahead in his Lotus. Then in the 20th lap, Lauda shot out of the bend that turns into the final straight and I realized that he had decided to overtake. This would not be easy, because Peterson was a tough nut. But Niki's determination was stronger and just before the righthand bend at the far end of the straight he got past his opponent. I was next to Beppe Viola who was giving a running-commentary. I whispered into his ear: 'Tell them that Lauda is a great driver – he really knows what he's doing.'

Lauda won, followed by Regazzoni and his ascent began.

In the afternoon, *Il Giorno* 'phoned me. Giulio Signori, head of the sports section, wanted a piece about the race. I 'phoned in a report, and the next day I sent another piece.

In the middle of October, I received a telephone call from Gozzi. He asked me if I could go to Modena on the 23rd. He was quite insistent. I confirmed that I would be available. I began to wonder what this could be about. None of my colleagues could enlighten me and no meeting or press conference was to be held on that day.

On the 23rd I arrived at Modena to discover the reason for the summons – I had won the Dino Ferrari Prize for Journalism. Many years had passed between the first one and the twelfth. The gathering was limited to the technicians from the factory and some colleagues from *Domenica Sportiva* and foreign television were also present. At a meal in the Tucano – the very place where Bandini had brought me to the encounter that occurred in 1963, – I was awarded the prize for the article I had written for *Il Giorno* after the Spanish Grand Prix entitled: *Una macchina che vola ha portato l'armonia* ['A flying car that brought harmony']. The sum was one million lire and I remember that, years before, I suggested to Ferrari that he should increase the prize from 500,000 lire to one million. When I received the envelope with the cheque and the small bronze of the Cavallino Rampante, I asked if I was expected to say a few words. Ferrari grimaced and said that I was not expected to, but that I could anyway.

The next day, very few papers reported the news of the prize. *Domenica Sportiva*, which had filmed the entire event, did not even transmit one second of it. It was the presenter who, after the report on Ferrari, mentioned on his own initiative that: 'The Dino Ferrari Prize for Journalism has been awarded to our colleague Gino Rancati.'

A few days later I received a copy of the film of the presentation along with the sound-track. I kept it and I have transcribed what I said directly from the tape: 'I am not expected to say a few words, but being so used to the microphone makes me feel obliged to. Some will be horrified by my winning this prize because, being a man of passion and intense feelings, I have also had disputes with Ferrari. These disputes arose from my affection for him and for the company he has created. I am standing here today (here my voice was cracked with emotion and I am not ashamed to admit it) on behalf of you engineers, mechanics and racing-drivers. I am here because on a happy day I was able to write a few words which, as always, came from my heart. We will gather together here again and it will surely be better than this year. This year, we have done a lot – I say "we", Ferrari, because the people who write or speak on Mondays, they too contribute something. I have a wish: that we will win, and that we will win with our hearts. One other thing. Before this prize-giving ceremony, I had the great pleasure of talking to my friends Bellicardi, Dondo and Pininfarina and we realized once again that it will be our hearts that will make us go far, make us win – you with your cars and we with our feelings.' In the film you can see Ferrari talking to Pietro Barilla just after my speech, but it is impossible to hear what he was saying. It's a pity; perhaps the great Ferrari was at this point explaining Rancati to his friend Barilla.

The million has not yet been spent, and is in a private account that Ferrari suggested.

So the Ferrari prize finally came to me, this gesture towards journalists being yet another means of satisfaction for Ferrari. There is no lack of ambitious people amongst motor-racing journalists and one person in particular is said to have cheated in order to win the prize. He even managed to get himself high level recommendations, but Ferrari would have none of it and apparently said that, whilst he was still alive, the person in question 'would only ever dream about the prize.' Perhaps this is why Giovanni Arpino and Alberto Bevilacqua, famous writers, won after me. The circle of journalists to whom the prize can be awarded has become smaller and smaller, so it has become necessary to turn to men of culture, to men who in the course of the past year have spoken about motor-racing, even if only once.

Enzo Ferrari
album

1930. Tazio Nuvolari: unrivalled in Enzo Ferrari's eyes.

1952. With Alberto Ascari, one of 'his' drivers.

MODENA **Ferrari** ITALIA

La « 166 Inter » vincitrice assoluta del 2° Gran Premio Internazionale di Torino di Km. 504 alla media oraria di Km. 108,825

1956. Dino's smile and a touching verse. (Translation on page 198).

1956. Ferrari with Luigi Musso, Eugenio Castellotti and Peter Collins.

Tu che dalla vita
che pur tutto poteva offrirti
ricevesti tanta sofferenza
Tu che sapesti accogliere
con ferma dignità umana e Cristiana rassegnazione
anche l'estrema rinuncia
alla Tua giovane esistenza
Tu che sapesti offrire la Tua lunga agonia
perchè più forti
potessero essere i Tuoi cari al momento
del gran passo della Tua dipartita terrena
dall'alto del regno dei Giusti
ove certamente l'Onnipotente ti ha posto
sorreggi tutti coloro che ti piangono
e sii di conforto per la Tua Mamma
e vivida fiamma sulla via che Tuo Padre
deve ancora percorrere
a maggior onore di quel nome che fu Tuo
e Tuo rimarrà

1958. The Modena track. On the right of Ferrari, Mino Amorotti, racing manager, and Luigi Bazzi.

1961. Gino Rancati interviews Ferrari in front of the first Maranello rear engined racing car.

Ferrari, a lonely man.

1961. Giancarlo Baghetti, the shooting star, in whom Ferrari sensed the presence of a champion, he later disappeared.

1961. Carlo Chiti persuading the *Commendatore* about the superiority of the rear engine.

1963. With Giancarlo Bussi and
Franco Rocchi at Monza, next to
a BRM.

1962. Driver, Willy Mairesse, tells Ferrari of his hopes.

1963. Enzo Ferrari and Lorenzo Bandini. Maurio Forghieri listens to John Surtees.

1965. The *Cavallino Rampante* lapel badge. Later he stopped wearing it.

1976. Niki Lauda, another of 'his' drivers, was later to abandon him.

1980. Ferrari gives Gilles Villeneuve the embrace he never allowed Tazio Nuvolari.

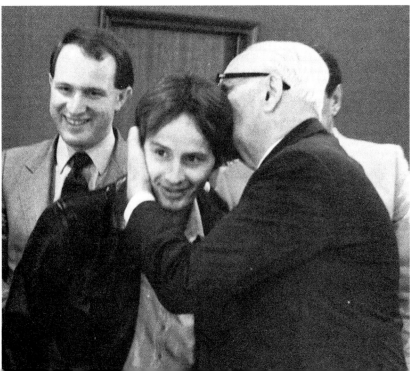

1964. Listening intently to Mauro Forghieri and Eugenio Dragoni.

1987. Piero Lardi Ferrari with his father who is listening intently.

1988. The last Grand Old Man.

19

Enzo Ferrari, inside and out

The 1975 world title meant that Ferrari gave his press conference on the Fiorano track and at the end of it he presented the new Formula 1 single-seater for the 1976 championship. During the repartee with the journalists, one of the young men asked whether Ferrari had ever thought of turning to politics? He replied resolutely: 'No, even though I have had offers. I should like to be an ambassador, so that I would not have to live in this country.' Everyone laughed. Despite his years, Ferrari was still very quick-witted.

Many people have asked me for whom Ferrari voted. Certainly for a centre party – even if once, according to him, the Communist party offered him a seat in the Senate. As a convinced nationalist, he could not wander too far from the positions he had taken. At Modena, some people say that Ferrari gave money to political parties, particularly those of the centre right. Is this true? He certainly belonged to that generation of men who bow their heads slightly when they say the word *'Patria'* [fatherland]. Remember Nuvolari and the Italian flag at the Nürburgring? However, in Ferrari's later years, I think that even the fatherland started to have less influence on his way of thinking. Still, Ferrari was an example of patriotism for many – one of those wholesome ones who work, who uphold the name of Italy before the rest of the world and who allow themselves no rest in their reaffirmation of their own work.

The 1976 world championship started with a supremacy that was perhaps too marked, but the Nürburgring accident would put the Ferrari company in the difficult position I have already described. When Lauda returned from Japan and the whole motor-racing world wanted Ferrari to say what he would do, he – understandably enough – did not know what action to take. He thought of issuing a communiqué in which he would suggest to Niki Lauda, his champion, that he should retire. There is no doubt that this would have been a wrong move. He mentioned it to someone from Fiat in Turin who told him not to do it, but to make a statement after he had seen Niki Lauda. He realized the false move he was about to make and he followed the advice.

Then he organized an immense press conference in which he spoke for hours and answered all questions. I was not invited and I was ready to bet that Gozzi would find the right lie in explanation, but I never asked the reason for this omission. Perhaps because I had placed myself outside his environment as far as my work was concerned, Ferrari did not consider it would be useful to invite an outsider.

On the 17th November, I received the following telegram: 'I should like to give you a copy of my latest book in which I have mentioned you and I should like to meet you for lunch on Saturday the 20th November as 12 o'clock in the Ristorante Fini, Piazzale San Francesco, Modena. Kind regards. Enzo Ferrari.'

On the 19th, I sent a message to Gozzi saying that I would not be able to be in Modena the next day. In the evening, I received another telegram: 'I have tried to speak to you three times on the telephone, but without success. Your secretary has informed me that you will not be able to come here tomorrow. I am very sorry, because I have held you up as the best of all. Yours, Enzo Ferrari.'

In his book, Ferrari had written about me as follows: '"You met me on the 26th January, 1956, at 10 o'clock," Gino assures me, displaying his usual amazing ability to quote dates. Everyone used to say what a fantastic memory he had, until his best friend – was it you, Athos? – began to cast doubts. The reputation of his memory did not collapse, but vague conjectures were made and the desire to check was aroused. On the TV he would commentate any sport in a free and easy manner. Once, in a live television commentary, he even permitted himself the luxury of criticizing a President of the Republic who was arranging his white hair at the Monza motor-racing track, after a 40 minute wait. What a dressing down! Another time, on my 70th birthday, he wrote that the Maranello lion "no longer roared, had lost his mane and presented a sad, outdated figure who was condemned to the archives." His criticisms are constructive in their exemplary destructiveness. His comments, which are just as corrosive, are quite instructive. He is fatalistic and passionate. He does not nurse lukewarm hates, but declares himself for or against with the same intensity, obeying emotional impulses that can make him sympathize with the Liberal Party or feel solidarity with the *Manifesto*.

'He seeks out good wines and sporting talents – especially footballers. One day he will be chairman of Juventus, he thinks, giving a perfect imitation of someone waiting for the offer that will make him happy. Boniperti has been warned.

'He writes a lot and well, but is spontaneously attracted to the microphone. When will Italian television give him the job that is his due, because he is the best of all?'

You were too kind, Ferrari.

I did not know where I wrote or spoke the words he attributes to me on his 70th birthday. But, since he put them in quotation marks, he must have had proof of them. It seemed strange to me that I could have spoken so ferociously about him. Perhaps I was subject to those 'emotional impulses' at the time?

Some time later, he told me that the quotation came from an article I had written for an RAI company magazine, a publication which he certainly did not receive. This was another of the man's strengths – he always knew everything. In this case, I think that someone must have sent him the magazine with the article.

Saying that I was the best of all was a true gift from Ferrari. I am one of those people who do not delight in commendations, who always earn the minimum, are 'difficult', say what they think in any circumstances, never do anything illegal and always pay in person. Many argue from morning to night to be able to work less, I have to argue to be able to work – and I hardly ever manage it. Great patience is needed.

Like Giovanni Drogo, the protagonist of *Il Deserto dei Tartari* ['The Desert of the Tartars'], I am waiting for the day I will be able to work in peace.

The meeting for the distribution of *Il flobert* occurred once again as a press conference in which the main subject of the questions was the Grand Prix situation and what was to happen in the future. There were many questions about Niki Lauda. Ferrari answered: 'We will know what condition Lauda is in when he is back with us, which we hope will be soon. In any case, even if he is not the same driver he used to be, we will all help him to find his feet again.' As Athos Evangelisti noted in the *Gazzetta dello Sport*, this was 'the reply of a gentleman'. The racing year was now over for the man from Maranello. He was sadly aware that the journalists would now leave him in peace for some time and he would miss the man-to-man contact, or the experience of addressing a group. This was a way of staying lively, a way of struggling, as he had always struggled. Winter was near and the fog would sometimes prevent him from going to Maranello, the centre of his world, where the GT cars for the wealthy were created but, more importantly, where the single-seaters were made that would allow Lauda and Reutemann to put the others in their place in 1977.

Ferrari's day always began early. For years, the first thing he did was to read the papers – seven or eight of them each morning. He was an attentive reader and his memory helped him to catalogue whatever would be useful to him in the future.

At eight o'clock he would go to the barber, Antonio, Franco Gozzi's father-in-law with whom he often had animated conversations – though there were often long silences as well. Then he would go to the cemetery. He once said: 'I am not an industrialist, but I give what is left of me to a small department of studies and advanced products, in the conviction that the results will be of use to the progress of automobile technology. At 78 years, this is the milk of my old-age. Each morning I get up with death in my heart.'

But one of his passions, which was as strong as his desire to win, was his respect for money, a respect he would never lose. The total income he had each year from the racing department was around three thousand million lire. Two thousand million came from Fiat, six hundred million came from sponsors (four hundred million from AGIP alone), another 400 million were collected here and there – for example, each Ferrari road car made was 'taxed' by a certain amount, which went to the racing department. Three thousand million is certainly not a little, even though running a team like the Ferrari one cost a great deal.

At the end of 1976, Fiat asked if it could put its logo on the single-seaters driven by Lauda and Reutemann. It was not easy to find the right place, partly because of a certain amount of resistance from Ferrari, but in the end, the inscription was placed on the sides of each car.

Two days before the Argentinian Grand Prix (9th January 1977), a report from Buenos Aires appeared in the *Gazzetta dello Sport*. 'The Fiat sign has appeared on Ferrari cars for the first time. The emblem of the Turin company is clearly visible next to the racing numbers. Fiat, who are co-owners of Ferrari, had always preferred not to appear officially, in order to avoid awakening public opinion to the involvement of the company in major motorsport competitions. The management of the Maranello company maintains that the Ferraris will carry the Fiat sign only in the two South American races, in order to satisfy a request from Argentinian and Brazilian agents of the Turin company.'

We may very well wonder whether Ferrari agents in other countries where Fiat sold its cars might have felt ashamed that the Ferrari company belonged partly to the Mirafiori company. It may also be thought that two thousand million lire was a high price to pay for the two signs on the sides of the Formula 1 Ferraris. What other advertisers could have been worth more to Maranello? Such an attitude on the part of the Ferrari company was absurd, after all what if someone in Turin had thought of removing all publicity from the Ferrari cars apart from the Ferrari logo, the Cavallino Rampante and the Fiat logo. If the dozens of signs previously carried only brought in 600 million lire, it would perhaps be advisable to cancel them and avoid the distraction they created. There is not a vast difference between two thousand million and two thousand six hundred million. The appearance of Renault in Formula 1 will tell us more about this.

As regards sponsorship income, I always thought that the dozens of signs that appeared on Formula 1 cars would have brought in more. Ferrari always said he only gave publicity to products that were directly connected with cars. He always maintained that publicity for cigarettes, perfume, etc never interested him. But someone has let it be known that, in 1971, he offered Ferrari money to be able to write the name of a cigarette on his cars. Ferrari refused, but according to this person, it was 'only because he wanted more money.' Can it be true?

Ferrari liked to make money – and who can blame him? – but he also liked to spend it. He personally saw to the gift items that were to be distributed to customers and friends.

A few years ago, he started sending sets of table linen which had been made especially for him, with the inevitable Cavallino Rampante. He had women's scarves designed according to his directions and in the colours he chose. But later he stopped giving gifts with the Cavallino Rampante emblem. He sent Lambrusco and *zampone* [stuffed pig's trotter] for Christmas. I once asked him why he chose this Emilian *charcuterie* and he replied, wittily: 'First of all because *zampone* is a Modena speciality and then because it allows me to give a piece of pig to someone and then to be thanked for it.'

Giovanni Agnelli also received *zampone* and Lambrusco. He told me that once the consignment was late and the lawyer himself has asked whether Ferrari had forgotten him.

Another idiosyncrasy of Ferrari's was that he claimed to keep his will and his accounts on two visiting cards which he kept in his wallet.

During the long days, which were interrupted only by visits from a few friends or from those that could be admitted to his presence, Ferrari dreamed of future encounters. Encounters with the men and the cars of his opponents. All in the name of sport and in the name of his unbroken will to win. About sport, he said: 'I believe in sport, because it has no limits, it transcends our own will and is an ideal that we have pursued and will continue to pursue. Because, if we forgot those who, in their eagerness to win, have given their lives, we would commit the most wretched betrayal, and the eagerness that up until now has guided us would become reprehensible and would make us unworthy of the consideration that I am shown every day.'

This is the image of a noble and ideal sport. But for Ferrari, sport – the sport of motor-racing – was above all an occasion to do battle, to show that he was the best and that he had dedicated his whole life – not just transitory passions – to this sport.

A strong leader of men and solver of problems, he spent fortunes on the factory, which he always wanted to be efficient, clean and well-lit. He prepared for every meeting as if it were an exam – he re-read the dates and the themes of previous meetings. He did not like to be caught unawares and he knew how to make full use of the fascination exuded by his personality. When the E Type Jaguar cabriolet came out, he told me he considered it to be the most beautiful car in the world, but then he also told me that he wanted a Rolls-Royce, but could not afford it. Every year he gave millions of lire to the Istituto Mario Negri in Milan for research into dystrophy, in memory of Dino. He continued to deny himself holidays and evenings at the cinema. He watched a lot of television – all the channels that could be picked up in Italy – and he was very proud of the audio-visual centre, worthy of a Head of State, that Ghedini had created for him at Fiorano.

Visits by the fair sex still excited him. There were always two aspects to his attitude to women: admiration and criticism. Although appreciating them, he considered them to be possible bringers of delusions and deceit – instruments of pleasure, and little more. How many times have I heard him say that when a man says 'I love you' to a woman, he only means 'I want you'? Many, many times.

Yet he never shunned the fascination of women, whether young or not so young. He also had 'something on the side', and not just when he was young. I think I can safely say that he considered women to be objects, as if they were something that could be completely owned. He was always very jealous and absolutist. When he was going to meet a woman, he always wanted to find out everything about her before seeing her so that he could let her know, at an opportune moment, that she could not make up stories about her past. He also amused himself by inserting something of what he had found into the conversation.

He quickly understood that he could not harbour any illusions about women, especially since he considered them to be creatures who had been put into the world to obey him. He liked to be gallant, to play the part of the cynic, of the person whom no one understands or of the man who is hardened to all the emotions and all the surprises that may arise from a meeting or from a moment of sincerity.

In his later years, he became closer to his wife, Dino's mother, than he had been before. She had been confined to bed for some years. She was not an easy woman, but she was very lucid and she took an interest in racing, wanting to know even the smallest of details.

He lived with her in the big building in the Piazza Garibaldi where, apart from their flat, there was the Ristorante Tucano and an office. There were dozens of empty rooms – they did not want anyone else.

Of the famous women who visited him at Maranello, he

remembered their beauty, their gentleness and the way they behaved with their men, all of which revealed their characters to him. He always watched for any sign of approval from these women – approval of his behaviour or his way of talking – and he always took great pleasure in a feminine compliment. Compliments paid to him by men, even famous ones, he could not so easily remember. If I had to pick two names that I heard him mention the most, I would say Ingrid Bergman and Anna Magnani. One for her tenderness, the other for her determination and both of them Roberto Rossellini's women.

'Anna Magnani,' Ferrari wrote, 'made a big impression on me. What a disconcerting woman! But she was not fond of speed, like Rossellini. I remember one day she came with me from Maranello to Modena. After a couple of long straight stretches of road, she asked me to slow down. It was not so much that she was afraid, she said, but that a strange feeling took hold of her every time the engine speed went to maximum revs. It was as if the roar penetrated her very bowels. Later I asked one of her friends what on earth this feeling could be and he explained it in the Roman dialect which, in its straightforwardness of language and its expressiveness, is really unsurpassable.'

But Ferrari also changed with growing years, at least partly. He became gentler and shouted less than before, but he still did not accept compromises. He was sorry that he could not speak English because he would have liked to give British constructors tit-for-tat in their own language when they made the pilgrimage to Maranello. He shouted less, yes, but I am sure that he always kept the list of people to 'bite' with him and that he never forgot it. Perhaps he dreamed of an absolute friend but he never allowed himself this pleasure because, with him, no one was allowed to go beyond certain limits. Here and there he found a moment of serenity but the thought of death never left him. He waited confidently to obtain some satisfaction outside the victories on the racing circuit.

Ferrari was still Ferrari – Ferrari with his legendary stable. Every day people waited outside the factory to see him and applaud him. They waited for hours and hours in front of Cavallino, they had a coffee and then went outside beneath the trees. When they saw him coming to the restaurant after one o'clock they would greet him with appaluse and say encouraging things to him. He would reply by raising his right hand, almost as if he were blessing them. This 'ceremony' would take place every day and he would expect it. Perhaps, though he never let it show, he was also moved by it.

I was certain that, before he died, he would leave some kind of written testament for someone. And here I found myself faced with the final dilemma – to whom would his fortune go, because it certainly was a fortune? I was sure that Enzo Ferrari's will would be a very great surprise.

I already knew one item of the will. I had suspected as much beforehand and it was confirmed to me on the 24th December 1976, when I telephoned Ferrari to give him the season's greetings. We were talking about one of his cousins, a very intelligent individual, who is one of the directors of the Istituto Mario Negri in Milan. This is Professor Mussini, who once told me an episode showing what a kind-hearted person Giovanni Borghi, the head of Ignis, was. Professor Mussini said: 'We are researchers in two different ways: we look for scientific solutions and we look for money. If our fellow-men do not help us, we cannot make progress and this is why we knock on every door to satisfy our needs. One day I went to Comerio to tell Borghi what we were short of. We needed refrigerators, washing-machines and some other things that he made. He listened to me attentively and then, in his quiet voice, he said: 'How many lorry-loads?' When I explained that we needed only four or five of his appliances, he was very disappointed.'

We were talking about the same Istituto Mario Negri, when Ferrari told me: 'When I die, they will get a lot.' He pronounced these words so distinctly that it was almost as if he was dictating them to me.

The times had long passed when, at the slightest upset, he would threaten to burn everything to ashes. The Grand Old Man had changed. Whereas before his aim had been to deride his fellow-men and to show them what he was made of, goodwill now seemed to be transforming him. Old age is a time for weighing things up, and he had been doing this for some time. He had discovered that love is stronger than hate and, in my opinion, it will be from love that the new Ferrari, the Ferrari of legend, will be born.

Saturday the 5th March, 1977. Niki Lauda had just won the South African Grand Prix. The champion had shown that he was worthy of trust, both as a man and a driver. My joy was as great as his and as great as that of the few people who always believed in

169

him. Ferrari had had the great Tazio Nuvolari and Achille Varzi at his court. As far as I was concerned, from that day the Austrian champion was called Tazio Achille Niki Lauda.

There was no need to pay attention to what people wrote and said. His 'backward steps' had been considered from all points of view and the accusations after Japan had been relentless. This great day was saddened by the death of Tom Pryce. It would be a nice gesture if Lauda dedicated his win to his poor British colleague.

What about Ferrari's attitude? I cannot avoid reproaching him somewhat. Was it possible that someone who knew men and racing-drivers as well as he did could not have completely understood the essence of Lauda? Had he been influenced by the mob (and let us take the mob to include certain sections of the press)? And what if Tazio Achille Niki Lauda, after his latest win, should fly into a tantrum? I did not think he would, he was too serious. But if he wanted to impose new conditions on his marriage to the Maranello 'belle' he would have good reason to do so.

On the 19th March, 1977, the Ferrari company circulated the text of a letter from Enzo Ferrari to the members of the board of directors. This is what it said: 'Dear friends and colleagues, I would like to inform you that, with the extraordinary meeting of the 5th March, I consider my task as chairman of the company to be over and I ask you to make provisions for the consequent changes. The re-occurrence of the professional illness that kept me absent for one month last January and the fact that on the 20th February I started my 80th year suggest to me that it is my duty to resign. The one who gave life to the Ferrari company and who wants it to continue to develop and to succeed, is very conscious of this duty today. I shall remain a member of the board and every remaining day of my life you will see me at Maranello, where I shall be available for anyone to whom I can be of use.

'There is no doubt that the new programmes we have just defined will require a commitment that I can no longer provide as I did in the past and for these reasons alone, I ask you to accept my resignation as chairman. My heartfelt thanks to you all. Enzo Ferrari.'

The 'professional illness' was said to be the sensitivity of his lungs to exhaust fumes and this peculiar affinity with Tazio Nuvolari was yet another bond between Ferrari and his favourite racing-driver.

170

As may well be imagined, the letter, which had been preceded by a leak to a Milan newspaper, gave rise to much speculation. On the 20th March, I sent the following letter to Ferrari: 'Dear Ferrari, So we have reached the penultimate act. The last act will be when you give up racing. Many of my colleagues are irritated by the news given by Benzing. I think he did well to get Sergio Pininfarina to talk. With Sergio in Geneva, we remembered our friend Ferrari, with Fusaro and Manicardi. None of us – not even remotely – allowed anything to be suspected. I do not believe the reasons for your retirement. Even if your health is causing you to suffer, you are not the one to back out. No doubt there is something else in it. Perhaps it would not be difficult for me to ask, but I prefer to stick to my opinion. I only hope that what I heard years ago (uselessness of cars like Ferraris, transformation into an engine factory, etc, etc) will not come to be true. And now, my dear Ferrari, I wish you peace. I will come to Maranello and we will talk about races and memories, but not about this "strange" decision. This time, will you allow me a strong fraternal embrace? You know how close to my heart you are. Many best wishes from your Gino.'

Once the letter had been sent, I thought that the readers of this book would perhaps want to know something more, so I made a telephone call. It seems that the letter was already on Ferrari's desk on the day that the name Fiat appeared next to the driver's name on the sides of the Maranello single-seaters in the world championship contests of Buenos Aires and Interlagos. This could mean that Ferrari could not have 'swallowed', as they say, the appearance of this other name. It also seems that Ferrari's resignation as chairman was part of a progressive abandonment of his commitment to the production of GT Ferrari cars and to Fiat.

But he remained in control of the racing stable and returned to being the authentic Ferrari – the sportsman, the skilful artisan and man who wanted to win on his own. I am certain that, if he could have, he would have bought back his factory. But this was no longer possible and so it was better to be an agitator, to stir up the waters and to be an awkward associate – polite, but intractable. Ferrari had started the 80th year of his life and, in my opinion, he was more than ever the great fighter that many of his opponents had known.

When would the next move be made?

20

1978: Ferrari becomes more alone

In April 1977, my original book *Ferrari lui* ['Ferrari, the man'] came out. On the 27th, I received this letter: 'Dear Signor Gino, I have read your Ferrari and I owe you an explanation. My father wrote with a copying pencil, because in those days the use of a letter-book was obligatory, and his signature would come out violet. My faithfulness to this memory will tell you why I use violet ink. All the rest is as you thought and sensed. When you come to reprint the book, I found an extra "that" on page 164. I don't know how many of us there are, but I am one. Best wishes.'

Typical Ferrari! He explains his violet ink to me, he points out an error (though I cannot see where there is one 'that' too many) and tells me that 'I don't know how many of us there are, but I am one', referring to the dedication in the book: 'To all my friends and thus to Enzo Ferrari also. But if he is not one of them, never mind.'

I wrote back, thanking him for his explanations and suggestions, and I added: 'There are few of us and I am glad that you have accepted – for many reasons. Now that I have my copy of Ferrari, I wish I had never written it. What can I say?'

One day, at a press conference, he said that millions of words had been spoken and written about him and that some had repented of what they had said. But I did not mean to repent.

Giovanni and Umberto Agnelli were among the people who received a copy of my book, and the former wrote to me: 'Dear Rancati, I have skimmed through your book about Enzo Ferrari. I shall later read it more attentively, but meanwhile I send you my congratulations for you have described the personality of a man who, like no other, has dedicated his life to engines and cars. Many thanks for the book and for the dedication and best wishes.'

My relations with the Grand Old Man continued to have their usual ups and downs. Sometimes we communicated and sometimes there was absolute silence.

Meanwhile, Niki Lauda won three world championship races, acquired more points and achieved his second world title. But at the end of the season, the Austrian left the Cavallino Rampante and joined Brabham. Later, Ferrari asserted that if Niki had stayed with him he would have equalled and perhaps beaten Fangio's record of five world titles. Ferrari was right.

On the 27th February, Ferrari's wife died in Modena. She had been born in Racconigi on the 10th September 1900. Ferrari wrote: 'I too have had a woman waiting in the pit when I was racing. She was my wife and she followed me everywhere. I lost her on the 27th February 1978 and I have made the bitter discovery of how the true value of the good things in life often becomes apparent when inevitable fate will no longer let us have them. She was a great help to me in what I might go so far as to call the heroic period of the Scuderia Ferrari.

'Her innate frugality, her desire to carry out tasks quickly, changes and agreements normally requiring time and reflection and her daily criticisms of my least decisions caused irritating disagreements, but also revealed the reality of such situations. For years, while I spent the entire day and much of the night seeing to the workshop, the office and the many needs of a small business she went around with my dear friend and collaborator Mino Amorotti from Avus to Le Mans, from Sebring to the Nürburgring – not so much to direct things but in the manifest conviction that her presence would mean substantial economies. We have been together for 60 years and the daily arguments have cemented this union, even if the harshness of our relations sometimes made us recognize the necessity of going our separate ways. But the love of cars and the feeling that they had brought us together have kept us united and helped to overcome all of life's adversities, even the tragedy of our son's death.

'In her last years, when she too had been hit by muscular dystrophy in her legs and confined to bed, she followed the Ferrari victories and defeats on television. She had given up the disagreements and arguments of the past, but her smile and her blue eyes told me all her suffering and all her great joy.'

I knew Ferrari's wife Laura very well and her husband's description of her is exact and allows a glimpse of the depths of a disconcerting personality. I remember when he and I would go up to their flat in the evenings for a rapid dinner which she had hurriedly and somewhat carelessly prepared for us. She would accuse us of not wanting to honour her cooking because we were going on to another meal where a mother and her son were waiting for us. Poor, dear Laura. In early March I went to see Ferrari, partly to examine the Fiat Ritmo which would later appear on the market. It was a delicate mission. Ferrari was waiting for me on the Fiorano track. He at once started speaking to me about his wife and said: 'Now that she has gone, I have lost a valuable reference point.' I found this sentence disconcerting, but it should not be forgotten that Laura was the mother of poor Dino.

I remember that once, during a meal, when we were around the table, Ferrari's wife attacked me about a personal matter. Her husband asked her to be quiet, to leave me alone and not to bother me. He defended me, shouting at her to be quiet. There were other people at the table in the Cavallino, and not all of them close friends.

In the summer of 1978, Giancarlo Bussi, a member of the famous technical threesome at Maranello (Forghieri, Bussi and Rocchi), was kidnapped while on holiday in Sardinia. Nothing more was heard of him. Perhaps he had been confused with a rich relative? Ferrari would make no comment about this. Later he wrote: '. . . nothing more was heard of Giancarlo Bussi, who was kidnapped in Sardinia.' No one ever knew if the Sardinian kidnappers asked him for a ransom.

Every now and then we exchanged telephone calls, cards and short letters. The 80-year old car-maker was still solid as a rock and had an impressive memory. On the telephone, his voice was shrill and lively. Ferrari, who valued food and drink so highly, made great sacrifices at meal times but he did not want to lose his intellectual vivacity. He needed to be lucid for his racing-cars, for his arguments with his colleagues and for his periodical duels with journalists.

In early August 1979, I received a hand-written note: 'Dear Signor Gino, My cross has become heavier. Come quickly to drink some iced rosé. Best wishes to all.'

I was frightened. That 'come quickly' sent a shiver down my spine. What if he was unwell? A few days later I was in Maranello. I found him strong and serene and very happy to give me some of his invigorating Lambrusco rosé. I went back to Turin feeling reassured.

Meanwhile at the end of July 'the President of the Republic of Italy granted the *Cavalierato di Gran Croce* [Knighthood of the Grand Cross], the greatest decoration in the Republic, to the car-manufacturer Enzo Ferrari for his achievements in the car industry and car-racing.' We can be sure that Ferrari was annoyed that his industrial achievements had been mentioned before his car-racing ones.

21

The desecration of Dino's grave

In early October, a terrible event befell the Grand Old Man. On the night of the 8th, some depraved individuals (who were never caught) desecrated the family tomb in the San Cataldo cemetery in Modena.

They broke the marble stone and opened the coffin and cut into the zinc lining. But someone or something must have disturbed them, because they ran off leaving a couple of plastic bags on the ground. The body, which was intact after 23 years, was not touched. The criminals obviously wanted to steal poor Dino's remains so that they could ask Ferrari for a huge ransom.

One newspaper said: 'Yesterday morning at around 10, Enzo Ferrari also went to the cemetery. He took this new blow in his solitary way, just as he had taken all the other misfortunes that have come his way. He made no comment and he would not speak to anyone on the telephone. He was seen entering the cemetery alone and came out with his right hand over his temples. He went straight to Maranello.'

Some time later, in a chapter of his memoirs entitled *Il prezzo della notorietà* [the price of fame], Ferrari wrote: 'I would never have imagined that the price of fame, which I had paid at every stage of my life, would also include the destruction of the tomb in which my son Dino was buried 23 years ago. After so many events, I feel alone and almost guilty that I have survived. Sometimes I think that sorrow is nothing more than an exasperated attachment to life in the face of the blinding fragility of existence.'

He always said that life was like a switchback – some ups and some downs. 1979 finished magnificently for the Grand Old Man:

the South African Jody Scheckter became champion of the world with the Ferrari company. It was the ninth time since 1950 that one of Ferrari's drivers had won the title.

On the 1st December, the 50th anniversary of the Scuderia Ferrari was celebrated at Modena. Ferrari said he felt honoured by the recognition he had received, but that he did not deserve it because he had only done what he liked doing. He added: 'Any praise should be given to my collaborators who have been able to interpret my ideas and demands. I am not a technician, I am an agitator of men. I have already reached the top of the hill and I know what is in store for me. I want to see two dreams come true: the first is that I should be able to work right up until the last day and the second is that the Italians should recognize themselves as all the sons of one mother – Italy.'

The first dream is the one he pursued most tenaciously and the second belonged to the melodramatic side of his nature, which came to the surface every now and then.

My visits and telephone calls became rarer. Between Ferrari and myself, there were no longer the arguments that had flavoured our friendship and there was nothing that could cause temporary upsets to our relationship. But though the contacts between us became less frequent, the affection remained. Old friends can go for months without talking to one another.

Ferrari's habits had also changed. At the end of the year, the Ferrari magazine stopped appearing. He revised and republished his memoirs. He included additional comments in them and made a few slight but essential changes. After the Dutch Grand Prix in 1981, a sports paper published the text of the telex that the phenomenal Gilles Villeneuve (his new quasi-Nuvolari) sent to Ferrari, in which the Canadian gave his opinion of the car. The same paper published Ferrari's reply, also sent by telex. It seemed improbable to me that Gilles dictated the message immediately after the race and that Ferrari immediately replied and, in any case, how could a paper, even an important one, have obtained copies of the two messages. Perhaps the Ferrari company had – and not for the first time – been showing favouritism towards one journalist, which I, and others besides, consider to be improper with regard to the rest.

In the middle of August, I went to Monza to do a report on the Ferrari company's preparations for the Italian Grand Prix. The day before I had telephoned Maranello and I had spoken to Piccinini's assistant (Piccinini was the racing manager) to ask for permission to make a report on the practice for the television news.

When I arrived at Monza, a polite and presentable young man came up to me and introduced himself. He was Calzavara, Piccinini's assistant. As we walked up to the pits, I told him that I did not believe that the telexes between Ferrari and Villeneuve could have been exchanged so quickly and that I did not agree with this manner of giving preference to one single paper and thereby deliberately snubbing the others. Calzavara assured me that the telexes had been authentic. I said to him: 'Well, since you at Ferrari have an indemnity for the lies you propagate . . .' I made the report and went back to Turin. On the 24th August, I received a registered letter sent from Modena on the 21st. It was from Ferrari. He said: 'Dear Rancati, Calzavara has informed me that you told him at Monza that my letter to Gilles was fabricated, because you do not believe that I could have been in touch with him as early as the Monday morning. I am sorry to find that my hopes of some consideration on your part have been misguided. However, I am enclosing the photocopies, with the dates of the telexes, not so that you will believe me, but to allow me to suggest to you that your independence of judgement should not go so far as to offend someone whom in the past you considered your friend. Best wishes.'

The lion could still roar when provoked.

The telex from Gilles showed what an extraordinary man this driver was. The clarity with which he explained to Ferrari why the car did not measure up to its opponents and the frankness with which he acknowledged his own mistakes ('I'm sorry about the damage, but I could not stop myself from going into the attack . . .') were disarming.

22

Gilles Villeneuve: another legend

T he young Canadian was making Ferrari re-live what he had experienced in the days of Tazio Nuvolari. His courage and his desire to be first took years off Ferrari. The Grand Old Man made a fuss of the young driver and hoped to be able to give him a car that would allow him to become world champion – even though he knew that Villeneuve would ask the impossible of his cars, which could go so far as to damage their performance.

When I read the Grand Old Man's letter, I decided to write an article for *Il Giorno*, to which I had once more started to contribute, after a couple of years contributing to *Corriere della Sera*. My permanent employment continued to be with RAI as it had been, uninterrupted, since 1954.

Then I changed my mind and thought of writing to Ferrari. Finally I decided to remain silent: ignoring him was the best way to annoy him. So I kept quiet, though it was an effort.

On 8th May 1982, the bright comet that was Villeneuve was extinguished. The Canadian died during trials on the Zolder track in Belgium, on the second day of practice for the Grand Prix.

The television images of the driver, still attached to his seat, flying out of his car and meeting his death on the protective fence around the track, shocked the world. Also shocking were the words of the commentator. He was almost rejoicing because the Ferrari's ejectable seat had worked, as if the single-seater were a fighter aircraft and forgetting that the cause of the driver's death was to be found in his sudden collision with the fence. If he had remained in his cockpit, he would very probably have survived. The commentator went on to talk about centrifugal force and fireproof helmets, but this was irrelevant. Gilles was unfortunately dead and the papers would be full of news and comments about this for days to come.

A few months before, my friend Ferruccio Bernabò, a correspondent for *La Stampa* and a leading motor-racing journalist, had written: 'It is no secret that Ferrari has always had a preference for combative drivers, who were in some cases capable of taking more or less calculated risks. The great model remains the legendary Tazio Nuvolari, whom many consider to be the greatest driver of all time, or at least among the half dozen greatest.

'It was perhaps for this reason, that he wanted to take on Gilles Villeneuve, who is a little like the Mantuan champion of the thirties. Because of this likeness, Ferrari forgives him – which in the past he was rarely disposed to do – for wrecking so many cars. But there is a difference: Nuvolari also used to take risks, if that was necessary to avoid being beaten by more powerful machines, but he wrecked very few cars: isn't that true Ferrari?'

What Bernabò says is true, but it is understandable that the Grand Old Man should want to compare Villeneuve to Nuvolari and that he should hope that he had found his successor. Although it might – perhaps maliciously – be thought that the Canadian had become an idol for the crowds and that his name had perhaps partly supplanted that of the man who had given him his mount.

But Gilles' death was another terrible blow for Ferrari.

Didier Pironi, another of his drivers, also gave Ferrari reason to hope he might win the world title. But a serious accident during the trials for the German Grand Prix on the Hockenheim track sent the French driver to hospital for several months. He had almost 20 operations and it seemed a little risky to assume that he would return to racing.

Ferrari remembered Villeneuve as follows: 'There are those who defined him as an aviator and thought he was odd. The day he left Snowmobiles to join my team, there was a chorus of criticism and when I compared him to Nuvolari some gave me a sharp response. With his generosity, with the destructive capacity he had when driving cars, grinding up differential shafts, gearboxes, clutches, brakes, he taught us what had to be done in order for a driver to be able to defend himself in an unforeseen moment. He was a combative champion and made Ferrari even more famous. I liked him.'

I may be wrong, but I think this is the first time the Grand Old Man said that he liked one of his drivers. Villeneuve was also a serious young man who was reserved and jealous of his feelings. When I went to interview him at his home in Montecarlo in June 1981, after two magnificent wins in the Formula 1 world championship, I brought presents for his two children Jacques and Melanie. When I had given these to them, he said 'merci' to me and stared at me as if I came from another world.

Maranello was still the racing capital. In the stormy and absurd world of the world championship, where the dollar rules, Ferrari was still the boss. When the car-constructors had to decide something, they came to see the Grand Old Man in Modena. As a mediator, he played what was perhaps a new role for his temperament – the role of a patriarch, but one who was ready to throw himself into the fray.

Suddenly there was a surprise announcement: Niki Lauda was returning to racing. Ferrari said: 'When he suddenly withdrew I said that he had performed an act of honesty and courage. Now he has shown that he has plenty of courage to spare.'

The news started to go round Italy that Ferrari might be made a senator for life by the President of the Republic, Sandro Pertini. He immediately said that it was the Ferrari company that should be rewarded and not him, he was only a worker who at the age of 16 had worked in the fire-brigade's lathe-operator's workshop in Modena. This too was something new.

Beneath this new modesty lay his feeling of remoteness from the rest of the world and his rejection of officialdom. I am convinced that even if the other Grand Old Man of Italy – President Pertini – had nominated him a senator, he would have refused. At the end of September 1982, I left RAI, where I had worked for 28 years. I joined the illustrious *Gazzetta del Popolo,* which had returned to the news stands after 13 months' absence caused by the usual Italian machiavellian political reasons.

My decision provoked comments, some of them salacious. 'A person like him, leaving RAI . . .' But I felt free.

The Grand Old Man quickly found out, but he pretended not to know to friends who spoke to him about it. Perhaps not even he believed it.

Then on the 7th November, I decided to write to him. He replied on the 17th: 'Dear Signor Gino, The door to Maranello has always been open! Best wishes.' Once again, he had used that 'open door' tactic of his. It was I who had become distant, not he who had shut himself away in his retreat.

Then I telephoned him and we agreed that I should visit him at Maranello.

23

No longer Maranello, but Fiorano

The visit took place on the 7th December. I described it in the *Gazzetta del Popolo* on the 6th January 1983. It was Ferrari's first interview in his 85th year.

I will talk about the interview later. I had not seen Ferrari for a couple of years. He was still the same, despite his age. He was lively, with a clear voice and his usual remarkable memory. Nothing that happened – near or far – escaped his attention.

Racing remained his burning passion. It was the only reason for his sacrifices, his fears and his hopes, even when things were going badly.

The production of the most sought-after GT cars in the world interested him much less than it did when he used to direct it alone. Before the agreement with Fiat, it had been an essential support for the scuderia, but not now. It was the Mirafiori firm that now gave him a substantial part – more each year – of what he needed. The rest came from sponsors from whom he had a matchless ability to extract quite staggering figures.

The Grand Old Man had left Maranello and transferred the scuderia's headquarters to the other side of the street, in the parish of Fiorano. It was a much larger building, plain, in square style. It was a headquarters which, when seen from the outside, gave no idea of what it contained. It was on an avenue named after Alberto Ascari. Ferrari's office had light blue walls and still contained the big photograph of Dino and a picture of a Ferrari in a race. It was a welcoming environment where I immediately felt at ease.

Next to the office was the room for press conferences, an arena where the fighter (he was also a fighter with words) would sometimes receive his journalist friends and enemies.

The office was just a few metres away from the track, that 'unrivalled laboratory for our experiments.'

Wherever you looked were signs of the care Ferrari always took in his 'things'. The outside walls were painted yellow – the colour of Modena – in various shades.

It was obvious that he had returned to his origins and was now alone in his stronghold. Getting into the scuderia was rather difficult. The men at Fiorano said that several visitors, even famous ones, had to wait for Ferrari to give the go-ahead before they could cross the threshold.

It was inevitable that I would compare this new stable with the old one in the Viale Trento e Trieste at Modena, or the one at Maranello. They seemed far away to me now. The workshop gave the same impression – it was also a gem, and was maintained like a top-class watchmaker's shop.

But what did Fiorano represent for its boss? He replied with carefully chosen words: 'The new office of the GES (*Gestione Sportiva* [racing management] as it has been called for decades) represents "the exclusive workshop for the design and production of cars intended for racing".' In other words, Ferrari was here and the Ferrari company was over there, only a few hundred yards away but an infinite distance nonetheless.

In his office he showed me a photograph taken in 1924 at Cremona, my native city, which then had what was probably the fastest street racing circuit in the world. The circuit had endless straight stretches and along one of them attempts were made to break speed records.

The photograph was taken during the first trials of what was to become the invincible Alfa Romeo P2, Vittorio Jano's masterpiece. Ferrari told me the names, jobs and titles of the various men and women standing around the red car, as well as the relationships between.

We did another round through the various departments, where I met old acquaintances. But everything had changed so much that I felt a pang in my heart. Where was the unforgettable, modest Ferrari workshop of those epic years?

Ferrari told me: 'It's always like a family here. Fathers, mothers, sons, in-laws, uncles – all of them feel at home here and their lives are also the life of the scuderia.

184

Then we talked of the illness that killed his son Dino and of how people were unaware of its seriousness. 'There are tens of thousands of people suffering from dystrophy in Italy and every year a large number of them die young. Why is so little known and why is more not being done for them?'

His eyes were still clear and his words precise. He made quick and, if necessary, forceful replies.

He would still get up at half past seven every morning and go to the barbers. He no longer went to the cemetery every day. 'Gino,' he said to me, 'health is precious and I can't risk catching a cold or the 'flu. But when I'm feeling well, then I go to the cemetery.'

He told me with a smile that they would call him from 'over there' when they had to acquire new and expensive machinery. 'So I ring up to get a discount and a rapid delivery. Today, 2,500 Ferraris are made every year. Far too many – 2,000 would be enough. A Ferrari should be longed for and dreamed for. You should have to wait for one like you wait for a star.'

He no longer had lunch at the Cavallino. There was a well equipped kitchen at Fiorano, within the area of the track, where an excellent cook would prepare suitable food for him. He ate very little. The day I went to see him, he had a slice of cured rump of pork ('in honour of Gino, who loves it'), a couple of spoonfuls of rice with the mushrooms he liked so much and some fruit. He no longer drank wine, but offered me Lambrusco. He turned to Gozzi – his press secretary, adviser and unrivalled guardian – and said: 'Since Gino likes wine so much, are you sure you have remembered to send him some for Christmas?'

I thanked him, but I did not mention the fact that I once used to get 72 bottles and now got only half that amount.

Each Friday he would subject himself to a series of tests. If everything was in order, he would treat himself to a good meal at Saturday lunchtime, finishing with whisky, which he always liked.

We spoke of many different things, but not about politics which at one time he used to discuss at length.

Meanwhile, on the track, Tambay was trying out a single-seater and Ferrari listened to the roar of his 'horses' and interpreted their cries. He was still a good conversationalist. We talked about drivers. He remembered the question Vittorio Valletta had asked him years ago: 'Ferrari, you spend a fortune on racing and on running a company which is the pride of Italy, how on earth do you manage to make a profit?'

After the meal we drank barley coffee and he explained: 'Real coffee is for Saturdays.' It seemed a long time since he would proudly tell me he had discovered some inn on the Apennines where there was first-rate ham or tagliatelle. In the evenings he would eat some fruit, read a little and watch some television. He would go to bed around one, sometimes later.

He was like a big oak tree, ancient, of course, but dominating everything around. I am sure that the secret of his strength was Fiorano, where he had gone back to being the Ferrari who became big and famous all on his own, where from his window he could see his cars being tested and where his son Piero would be able to continue to develop his father's incomparable creations.

Years before, he had talked of death, saying that he got up every morning with death in his heart. Now he talked of the future – a future called 'racing'. I saw that he would like to go on talking but I had also noticed that he was slightly tired and in any case it was getting foggy.

It was time to ask him about the interview. He replied decisively: 'Only a written one, Gino, written questions and written answers. I have decided to apply this rule to everyone and I am sorry that it also has to be so for a friend – and a friend I trust. But I can't go back on one of my decisions. Give the questions to Gozzi and I will answer them.'

Then he said: 'Gino, no hyperbole, I implore you. Talk about this day we have spent together in the same way you used to describe a race or a new car – with the same clarity and simplicity you have used in nearly 30 years of television. In other words, with objectivity and not too many adjectives. Agreed, Gino?' 'Agreed,' I replied.

We embraced and I slipped into the fog – that old companion of us inhabitants of the Po valley. On the 30th December, I received a hand-written note from Ferrari: 'Signor Gino, In accordance with instructions to Gozzi, express delivery of the interview. Best wishes.'

Of the nine questions, I will select three.

First question: 'Could there ever be another Gilles Villeneuve in Grand Prix racing?' Reply: 'It would not be easy, since in addition to natural talent, whoever it was would have to have Gilles' relentless yearning to win.'

186

Second question: 'Is it true that you would like to have Alboreto in the team in 1984?' Reply: 'I have said before, and I will say it again, that if Alboreto were free I would be happy to put a single-seater at his disposal.'

Third question: 'What would happen if there were no more so-called sponsors?' Reply: 'If the Ferrari company lost its technical sponsors, that would mean that racing no longer interested them in that it had turned into nothing more than something to watch, and this would also mean the end of motor-racing. If on the other hand we take the word sponsor to mean the companies that have nothing to do with the technical evolution of the motor-car, it is obvious that eclipse would cause a difficult financial situation in some teams. However, technical research would continue and, with it, the future of motor-racing would be assured.'

In 1984, Michele Alboreto, a driver from Milan, born on the 23rd December 1956, joined Ferrari and with him the Frenchman René Arnoux. The Grand Old Man had thus gone back on his resolution never to have any more Italian drivers in the team, because of the invariable response of the newspapers, radio and television following an accident or death. But it seems that the 'associates' in Turin insisted. Ferrari with at least one Italian in the team attracted greater sympathy and improved the image of the team. I remain of the opinion that, quite apart from the undeniable qualities of Alboreto, Ferrari would have continued to ignore Italian drivers. But, as we know, technical associates-cum-sponsors also have their rights and this is inevitable in view of all the money they dispense.

Meanwhile, at the end of 1983, the *Gazzetta del Popolo* closed down. This was a hard blow, not only for the editorial staff, but for the whole of the nation's press and we who were out of work received many words of solidarity, though they led to nothing.

I was saddened, above all for the talented young people, of whom there were plenty in the editorial staff, especially in the sports section. I wrote to Ferrari: 'It's a defeat.' He replied on the 27th January: 'Dear Signor Gino, I know from cruel experience the cost of always saying what you think and believe in. I can easily understand your thoughtful state of mind, but do not give in! Thank you for your confident trust in me. Best wishes.'

On the 29th August, Ferrari held a hurried press conference.

Since I was not directly concerned with motor-racing, I was obviously not invited. But I wrote something in *Il Giorno*.

This was about sponsorship. Ferrari only accepted sponsors if they were of a technical nature. This time a cigarette manufacturer was 'offering' him drivers, apparently for a figure of around eleven thousand million lire.

Then I disclosed that, some months before, Niki Lauda had been received in Turin by one of the main representatives of Fiat. The meeting, for reasons of secrecy, was held in the offices of Cinzano in Via Gramsci. As is well-known, Cinzano is a company belonging to the Agnelli family. It seems that the man from Fiat asked the ex-driver to return to Maranello. The reply was said to be affirmative.

The Grand Old Man – one of whose most effective weapons has always been information – obviously found out about this meeting and during the press conference, he suddenly announced that his drivers for 1985 would be Alboreto and Arnoux. There was nothing to object to in this choice, but it was clear indication that he was still in command at the scuderia Ferrari and that no one else could interfere. And this is what I wrote in *Il Giorno*.

On the 31st August, I received a letter from Fiorano: 'Dear Signor Gino, I have read *Il Giorno*. It is clear that you have written what you think and believe to be true, as is your right. I enclose a copy of what I said. Read it and then examine your conscience. Kind regards.'

Further letters and notes expressing best wishes and greetings then followed at various intervals.

On the 28th August 1986 I went to Fiorano. Time was slipping by but the Grand Old Man was shouting almost as much as he used to. He was angry with the engineer Mauro Forghieri, who was guilty of having lost a good many technicians from his department. Ferrari told me: 'Almost all of them have left. It's quite incredible. All that skill and experience lost. I don't know how to describe such behaviour.'

I tried to speak about something else and he appeared to listen to me, but then he re-exploded into further shouting. Then he told me that he had sent Forghieri to the Ferrari engineering section which is in one of the buildings on the outskirts of Modena, on the road that goes to Maranello and then to the Apennines. I was surprised by the continual, violent attacks on Forghieri. Ferrari had turned into a terrible god, spouting curses. He returned to his victim several times over lunch. What was the explanation for this? The answer is straightforward: he felt betrayed by one of his people, one of his own creations.

Meanwhile, the other Grand Old Man of Italy, the President of the Republic Sandro Pertini, had gone to Maranello and to Fiorano to visit the Ferrari company and to see Enzo Ferrari. He arrived in a Maserati, though this was not deliberate. Alessandro De Tomaso, head of the illustrious Casa del Tridente, had managed it because the Maserati range included a four-door saloon, a suitable car for delegations. Ferrari glanced at it, muttered something to himself, but he no longer had the time or the desire to reveal his annoyance.

On the 4th June 1987, I was at Fiorano. *Auto Oggi*, a Mondadori weekly, was preparing to publish my short history of the world championships won by Ferrari. This history was to be preceded by an introduction containing a few questions put to Ferrari himself.

We were together in his office, talking about the latest novelties. He was just the same – a lucid mind, an impressive memory – an extraordinary and unique man.

Suddenly he said to me: 'Gino, everything that is here is mine and later it will be Piero's. This is the Ferrari works, where racing-cars are born. We are struggling, we cannot pin down the – often mysterious – faults in our cars. Sometimes they seem to have been caused deliberately: but there is still time. All this, I repeat, is ours. And if I could, I would even buy back the factory. When I handed it over in 1969, I did it because I was afraid I would die – fear made me take that big step.' I had the impression that someone, someone close to him was not telling him the truth.

While we were having lunch, the Ferraris were having trials at Imola. The telephone rang. Ferrari grabbed hold of the table and stood up (I could not understand where he got all his strength from) and started towards the telephone. Piero got there before him and answered.

The television, in keeping with an old habit, was on. Every now and then he looked at it, perhaps managed to catch a few sentences, then turned back to his guests. I was the only 'outsider'. As always, he had put me at the head of the table. He was on my right, with Piero by his side. Opposite were Piccinini and Gozzi. Piccinini talked knowledgeably about the stock exchange, shares, and the world of finance in Italy and abroad. To me he seemed more like the financial advisor to a world leader than Ferrari's racing manager.

The moment came to leave Ferrari. We embraced and then I went into Gozzi's office. Gozzi informed me that Razelli the general manager was waiting for me. I went to see Razelli and formed an excellent opinion of him. He was a Ligurian of few words, but the words he did use were as clear as his ideas. He showed me the new Ferrari which would be presented at the Frankfurt motor show. It was eagerly awaited. I asked him what its name would be. 'We haven't decided yet,' he replied. 'We've got two or three possible names. How about you, what would you call it?'

I replied that since Ferrari's biggest market was the United States and since it was now forty years since the first Ferrari car had appeared, it should have an English language name, for example 'Ferrari Forty'.

In early October, I received a beautiful silver plaque with the inscription: 'To Gino Rancati for a brilliant idea.' On the left was a black Cavallino Rampante and on the right 'F40 June 1987' had been inscribed. 'F40' was the name of the new Ferrari, which caused a real stir at the German show.

The plaque was accompanied by this letter: 'Dear Rancati, With this plaque I want to commemorate our meeting on the 4th June when you kindly contributed to the choice of name for the GT car we presented at the Frankfurt motor show. Your contribution has produced excellent results – the 'F forty', based on the idea of forty years of Ferrari cars, identifies and personalizes the fastest Ferrari GT. Kindest regards. G.B. Razelli.'

Next to this, on the left, was some slightly shaky writing in violet ink: 'To Signor Gino, Ferrari.'

I was reminded of the time years before when Lamborghini took my advice and called his GT car 'Espada'. Somewhere I must still have the telegram of congratulations which he and Nuccio Bertone signed as well as the strip of wood with its steel plaque bearing the word 'Espada' – the same strip of wood that was put on the sides of the car.

Every now and then I rang up Gozzi and received greetings from Ferrari. We exchanged notes. He no longer wanted to write long letters.

I realized that the Grand Old Man, surrounded by a screen which, out of respect, I did not try to penetrate (though I would perhaps have succeeded), was slowly giving up. This made me feel very sorry, especially since I had often been rough, cruel and mischievous towards him.

I wrote to him on his 90th birthday (18-20th February 1988). He replied by typewriter: 'Thank you for your greetings. Best wishes.' 'Dear Signor Gino' had been written at the top in a steady hand and his signature was at the bottom. The event was celebrated by a lunch for all the Ferrari company.

The University of Modena awarded Enzo Ferrari a degree in physics. He therefore now had two honorary degrees, but, though he was pleased by this homage from his city, Ferrari no longer attached much importance to it. In Lugo di Romagno, Francesco Baracca's birth place, he was also granted the freedom of the city, but even this did not over-excite him.

His racing-cars were what mattered and Berger's wins in the last two Grand Prix races of 1987 gave him renewed hope, even though he knew that the path ahead was difficult.

I could have asked Gozzi or Piero to tell me more, but I thought this would be a violation of the cloistered life my friend was living.

Piero married Floriana when he was young and they had a daughter, Antonella, who was now twenty. She in turn had a son, who was given the name Enzo. So Piero, then not yet 43, was a grandfather and Ferrari a great-grandfather. When Antonella was born, Gozzi rang the Commendatore from the clinic to give him the happy news. Ferrari asked: 'Is it a boy or a girl?' When he heard the word 'girl' he muttered 'Ah!' and Gozzi realized that he would have preferred a boy.

24

Last chapter for the Grand Old Man

On Friday the 3rd June 1988, the papers had headlines saying things like: '*Pope at the court of King Enzo*'. And indeed, on the next day. John Paul II went to Maranello and Fiorano to meet Ferrari. What I had predicted had come true. But considering what a male siren the Grand Old Man was, it was an easy prediction to make.

On the evening of the same Friday, my boss and old friend Giulio Signori rang me from *Il Giorno*. He said that the rumour was going round Milan that Ferrari was dead and told me to contact the scuderia or the factory.

I did not feel like doing it. I was afraid. If the rumour was true, a whole part of my life would have disappeared. I sat staring at the telephone for ages, but I could not bring myself to do it. Then duty prevailed, as is right. I rang Gozzi. After a short pause, I heard his voice: 'It's not true, Gino. He has not been well, as you know, since that attack of influenza in the winter. They may have fed him too much trying to get his strength back and his kidneys are feeling it. He has ups and downs. I don't think he'll be able to see the Pope. Don't worry, he'll get over it. Do you remember two years ago at Easter, when he seemed to be about to die? Then he opened his eyes, looked at us and said: "I'm still here". Don't worry.'

On the Sunday, the papers, radio and television all reported the Pope's visit to Fiorano. But Ferrari stayed in bed in Modena. Piero stood in for him. He drove the Mondial cabriolet and John Paul II stood in it, without any protective glass, as Piero drove him among the workers and around one lap of the track.

After the heart-warming visit, the Pope telephoned Ferrari from

Fiorano. What can they have said to one another?

His father had barely left, as they say, and already there was murmuring that Piero was about to leave the racing management (the famous GES) of which he was the manager. Only a short while ago he had been greeting the Pope with the chairman Vittorio Ghidella and the staff of the factory.

These rumours were not new. The first signs of the possible move had already made themselves felt after the Mexican Grand Prix a few days earlier, at the end of May.

Piero declared: 'It is not true that I have quarrelled with my father. We have different points of view regarding the employment of John Barnard. He is in charge of the team and he will decide. The word 'he' referred to his father, of course.

Ghidella said: 'Don't ask me. On the 8th of June there will be a board meeting at Ferrari's and we shall see. I don't think anything will change. Barnard is the technical director.'

In my opinion, everything had already been decided. Some alliances within the racing section must have broken up – the alliances that had led to the removal of Mauro Forghieri in June 1987. The person pulling the strings was still the same – a young man who knew about finance. Let no one hold it against me if I am wrong, but my intuition suggests to me that what I have said is true.

The situation was not calm and neither were the drivers. Berger would remain for 1989, while Alboreto might leave, possibly to be substituted by Nigel Mansell, the Englishman who, in 1986 did not behave very properly towards the Ferrari company. He signed for 1987 but later withdrew.

Surprising announcements continued to come out of Modena and its Ferrari annexes. On Monday the 6th June, I read that Ferrari had been converted and that he had made his confession one month before. The day before the Pope's visit, he was also said to have taken Holy Communion.

I do not believe this. If he did take Holy Communion, perhaps he was not completely conscious. Those who know what happened will be able to judge my opinion.

Don Sergio Mantovani, the drivers' chaplain and a friend of the Ferrari company, said: 'There is nothing strange in the idea that Ferrari should have made his confession one month ago and taken the Eucharist the day before the Pontiff's arrival, although I would be interested to know how certain journalists obtained such private and personal information.'

On Wednesday the 8th June, *La Stampa,* the Agnellis' daily paper, said that Ferrari was ready to cede to Fiat his 40 per cent share-holding in the Modena factory. The remaining 60 per cent belonged to Fiat (50 per cent) and Piero Lardi Ferrari (10 per cent). The Turin paper continued: 'No matter how things turn out, the racing department will remain the province of Commendatore Ferrari, according to an old agreement between the associates. In other words, Enzo Ferrari will remain the reference point as far as racing is concerned, even if he cedes his entire share-holding to Fiat.'

Thus, from 'owner and sole manager', the Grand Old Man would become a 'reference point'.

If he was able to resist the advance of time, it was only because he continued to be the leader of the GES. This was the only 'mission' left to him. He didn't care about the rest.

Thursday the 9th June. *La Stampa:* 'Piero Lardi Ferrari, son of the 'Drake' has been nominated vice-chairman of Ferrari Spa [*Spa* = joint-stock company]. This was the only piece of news to emerge from the shareholders' meeting held yesterday at Maranello. The transfer of shares (from Enzo Ferrari to Fiat) will be discussed later.'

'I do not exclude the possibility,' said Vittorio Ghidella, chairman of Ferrari Auto Spa, 'that Enzo Ferrari is considering ceding his share-holding. But I cannot say either way because I am not inside his head.' Ghidella went on to say that the shares held by Ferrari amounted to 40 per cent and that Piero had 10 per cent, while the rest were controlled by Fiat.

'At the moment,' continued Ghidella, 'he has ceded nothing and in any case all discussion about to whom he will cede it is pointless, since the agreement between Fiat and Ferrari obliges Ferrari to sell only to Fiat and obliges Fiat to buy.'

Ghidella also said: 'The Grand Old Man has complete authority in the racing section and we all hope for good results. There can be differing opinions in all families, but there are no quarrels. Piero Lardi has matured as a manager. After many years experience in the racing section, it was time for him to turn his hand to other things, to the overall management of the company.'

As always, Ghidella's words were clear, and anyone who wished to understand could do so. Before the share-holders' meeting, the chairman of Ferrari had been to see the honorary chairman at home in the Piazza Garibaldi.

By moving Piero to the factory, they were taking away his responsibility for the GES. This was the first step in an operation that had begun some time ago. Fiat wanted to take over the racing section too. There were various reasons why it did this: partly for the money the department was costing it and partly because the present single-seaters left something to be desired. There was also the fact that, in the eyes of the world, Ferrari also means Fiat.

It makes me smile to think of the time when the Grand Old Man was asked how much the financial contribution of the Mirafiori company to the racing department was worth. He replied: 'You have known it for years: 500 million per year, non-index-linked.' Perhaps the contribution started at 500 million, but it gradually increased to some tens of milliards.

I thought of my old friend and his state of mind. He must have felt he had his back to the wall. He was losing his scuderia and he knew it. Decades of struggle, sacrifice, bruising defeats and exhilarating wins were coming to an end. Years of glory were gradually disappearing as he faded.

I wanted to telephone him, but even if he replied, I felt he would not let me speak about the matter.

On the 22nd June, the following announcement was made to the world from Fiorano: 'Dr Pier Giorgio Cappelli has today started working with the Ferrari company. Though Enzo Ferrari is remaining in charge, Dr Cappelli will assist him in running the GES. The organization of the department will be as follows: Marco Piccinini, racing manager, delegate to international organizations, relations with the press on the racing track; John Barnard, technical manager; Guido Castelli will work with John Barnard on the developmental programmes for the cars. Harvey Postlethwaite has been entrusted with the development of the production F40 and the racing F40 Le Mans. Dr Pier Giorgio Cappelli was born in 1942 in Pavia, has a degree in physics and is married with two daughters. He has worked with the Centro Ricerche Fiat, Fiat Auto, Magneti Marelli and Alfa Romeo, both in Italy and in the United States. The engineer Pier Guido Castelli was born in Turin in 1947, has a degree in mechanical engineering and is married with two daughters. He has worked mainly with the Centro Ricerche Fiat. Maranello, 22nd June 1988.'

Little information could be extracted from this communiqué. Cappelli was to co-manage the scuderia with Enzo Ferrari and Castelli was to work alongside the technical manager, John Barnard. Fiat was inevitably starting to control the Cavallino's destiny in the racing department too.

The communiqué was followed by the dismissals of various technicians, who joined those who had already left. Austrians, Englishmen, Frenchmen – by this time, the scuderia had become the motor-racing equivalent of NATO. But not even this cosmopolitan team had managed to bring the world title back to Italy. Even the reliable Alboreto left, to be substituted by Nigel Mansell. The Turin company was tightening its grip. This was the least that could have been expected.

Barnard set about supervising trials for his single-seater with a 3500cc normally-aspirated engine designed for the 1989 championship, when turbo engines will no longer be permitted. The first 'official' appearance took place far from curious eyes. (There is never a shortage of onlookers when a Ferrari is roaring around the track at Fiorano.) The Alfa Romeo track at Balocco is more 'secret' and less accessible.

This marks another break with the past, but an indispensable one. Two different courses provide a greater level of experience.

I telephoned Gozzi. We exchanged a few words about Ferrari's health and agreed that I should go to see him in Fiorano as soon as I could. Meanwhile, the Modena *aeroautodromo* was no more, it had been demolished. The scuderia in Viale Trento e Trieste had been knocked down and a large building will take its place. On the ground floor, there will be shops and on the first floor will be the Ferrari offices, so as not to have to change the registered office, address, letter-headings, etc. The Ferrari family lived on this first floor for decades and Dino died in one of those rooms. The upper floors of the new building will house an immense private garage. Modena needs it too. The property is owned by Piero. In the meantime, some were wondering what had become of 'Ferrari Motor England' which the Grand Old Man is said to have formed in order to make it the last refuge for the scuderia. Did he want Piero, his successor, to be able to start up in the green of the English countryside?

I have always thought that he would be able to devise the most unimaginable scheme in order not to have to hand over his creation

196

and thus reaffirm his total independence. At the last press conference for the Formula 1 journalists, Ferrari 'forgot' to invite the correspondent from *La Stampa*, the Agnellis' newspaper. I am certain that my young and upright colleague, Cristiano Chiavegato, could not have committed any 'offence' against Ferrari. But for the Grand Old Man, being able to show that the scuderia was still his domain and that he could invite whom he wanted, was like a breath of fresh air. Many years had passed, but when he could play a little trick, he became young once more, like a boy who won't lend his toy to a friend. The *aeroautodromo*, the scuderia in the Viale Trento e Trieste, his son – and, despite what Piero said, the dispute was said to have been bitter – leaving the racing section to join Ferrari Automobili, all these changes were indications of a past that was disappearing. Who can tell whether the Grand Old Man realized this completely? The giant who had wanted to perform like one of his cars was gradually crumbling away. Each moment meant one less breath. Ferrari, who would have liked to 'fly' like his Gilles Villeneuve, was suffering the same agony as his Tazio Nuvolari.

Thursday 21st July. A newspaper headline: '*Enzo Ferrari in very serious condition*'. The doctors said that we could only hope. He was put on dialysis in his home. Ferrari had refused to go to hospital, just as I would have sworn he would.

In the house in the Largo Garibaldi, where for several years now Piero had been living above his father's flat and his mother had been living on the third floor, there was still hope. Was the heart of the most feared lion of the motor-racing world about to give in?

In my opinion, he had already given in when he 'lost' – if he even knew it – his scuderia. It was an inevitable loss. It happened when a man from Fiat, whose great merits and disarming frankness I hold in high regard, declared: 'The time has come when Ferrari has realized that there will always be a Ferrari company, even without Signor Ferrari.' That was the 4th July 1988.

On that day, my old and incomparable friend said goodbye to me.

Dino's Verse

You who suffered so much from life, which could have given you everything,
You who knew how to accept with the strength of human dignity and Christian
resignation even the great sacrifice of your youthful existence,
You who knew how to offer up your long agony so that your loved ones could be
stronger when you took the great step of disappearing from this world, from the
heights of the Kingdom of the Just where the Almighty certainly has placed you put
right all those who grieve over you and be of comfort to your mother and relight the
flame over the path that your father must still walk to the greater honour of the
name that was yours and that will remain yours